THIS GOD WE SERVE

Names and Characteristics of God

2nd Edition
Rev. William J. Morford

This God We Serve and other True Potential books can be purchased in bulk by churches, ministries and other organizations for evangelical, educational or business promotional use. For information please write Special Markets Department PO Box 904 Travelers Rest, SC 29690 or send your request via e-mail to: info@tppress.com.

Receive your FREE e-version of William Morford's book:
God's Rythm of Life: Seasons of The Lord. Understanding the
Jewish Roots of the Church.
Visit: www.OneNewManBible.com/Seasons

DEDICATION

This God We Serve is dedicated first to the Living God, Who desires and encourages relationship with Him for each one of us, to bring us into His Presence continuously.

This book is dedicated second to the Loving God, Who brought my second wife, Gwen, into my life after my first wife, Jeanie, died. Gwen greatly encouraged me for five years while I was completing the *One New Man Bible*. Gwen has been a wonderful help in preparing this Second Edition of *This God We Serve.*

TABLE OF CONTENTS

INTRODUCTION

Our Heavenly Father wants each of us to be on intimate terms with Him. We are told in Jeremiah 9:22. *Thus says the LORD*, **Do not let the wise man boast in his wisdom! Do not let the mighty man boast in his might! Do not let the rich man boast in his riches!** 23. But the one who boasts will boast in this, that he understands and knows Me, that I AM the LORD* Who exercises loving kindness, judgment, and acts of loving kindness in the earth, for in these things I delight, says the LORD*.*

May this book help you to understand and know Him in ever increasing measure and for your relationship with Him to grow day by day, becoming more intimate with each step in your spiritual growth. As we walk in relationship with Him we have to bear in mind that He is not limited as we are, because nothing is too difficult for Him, nothing is impossible for Him. *Is anything too hard for the LORD*? (Jer. 32:17, Matt. 19:26, Luke 1:37) At the time appointed I shall return to you, about this time next year, and Sarah will have a son.* (Genesis 18:14)

I know that You can do everything, (Matt. 19:26, Luke 1:37) and that no thought can be withheld from You. (Job 42:2)

Ah Adonai, LORD*! Behold, You have made the heavens and the earth by your great power and outstretched arm, there is nothing too hard for You. (Jeremiah 32:17)

What I am saying to you in the darkness, you must now say in the light, and what you are hearing in your ear you must immediately proclaim on your roofs. (Matthew 10:27)

If we are to have a relationship with Him, we ought first to meditate on what He expects of us. A number of verses give so much that books have been written on the subject, but Micah 6:8 tells us in answer to verse 7's question about offering his firstborn son; *He has told you, O man, what is good. **And what does the LORD* require of you, but to do justice, to love loving kindness, (1 Cor. 13:3-7) and to walk humbly in purity with your God?!*** (Deut. 10:12,13)

We are told in Matthew 25:34; *Then the King will say to those on His right hand, 'Come, the blessed of My Father, you must now inherit what has been prepared for you in the kingdom from the foundation of the world. 35. For I was hungry and you gave Me to eat, I was thirsty and you gave Me to drink, I was a stranger and you took Me in, 36. and I was poorly clothed and you clothed Me, I was sick and you visited Me, I was in prison and you came to Me.' 37. Then the righteous will answer Him saying, 'Lord, when did we see You hungry and we fed You, or thirsty and we gave You something to drink? 38. And when did we see You a stranger and we took You in, or poorly clothed and we clothed You? 39. And when did we see You sick or in prison and we came to You?' 40. Then the King will say to them, 'Truly I say to you, in so much as you did anything for one of these, the least of My brothers, you did it for Me.' (See Isaiah 58:6-10)*

To please God we must 'Love our neighbor as ourselves' as we are instructed in Leviticus 19:18.

We can see that God desires for each of us to walk in relationship with Him, truly doing all each one can to emulate Him, keeping pure, and loving our neighbors as ourselves. This relationship requires first that each one commit personally to Him, determined to do His perfect will, to change behavior, improving day by day. It is only when we change that others who know us can see that our commitment to God is real. The things we do speak louder than the words we speak. We show more of our relationship to the Lord by what we do than by what we say. Take the passage from Matthew 25 to heart and give evidence of your walk with God. Then get to know the Living God, the King of the Universe, in a very personal way. The King of the Universe wants to walk with you all day, every day, wherever you go, whatever you do. As we sing in the hymn, "..He walks with me and He talks with me.."

The book, This God We Serve, is the result of a personal desire to know God, to find out all I could about Him, our Creator. A good example of His being with us is His repeated use of the verb "to come." With Noah, He said "Come into the ark.." (Genesis 7:1), and with Moses He said "come" to Pharaoh each time Moses was sent to him. To the children of Israel He spoke of coming into the Promised Land. (Deuteronomy 26:1) God never told anyone to GO on a dangerous mission, it was always COME, to indicate that the Divine Presence was with the one sent. The Hebrew verb for come is BO, which is sometimes mistranslated as go.

As we read Scripture, we find not only God's plan for our lives, but we come to know Him in a personal way, to see His concern for His people, for each one as He walks with different personalities in Scripture. This book is a collection of words and phrases that describe God Himself. In the Scriptures quoted here, you will find that our Heavenly Father is very loving, more merciful than we can imagine. There is a tendency of some to focus on His anger or wrath more than love, mercy, and grace, but this study brings out that the preponderance of these characteristics are of His love and His desire for an intimate relationship with each one of us. Elihu's speech in the 37th Chapter of Job and Job's speech in the 38th Chapter express their feelings that God's ways are beyond human understanding, a feeling we all share. However, God wants all of us to understand and know Him (Jeremiah 9:23), with the goal of this study being for all who use this to come to understand and know more of Him. God said, And to man He said, *Behold, the reverence of the LORD*, that is wisdom, and to depart from chaos is understanding.* (Job 28:28)

In this study it is necessary to go to the Hebrew and Greek texts because many of the names for God are lost or obscured in making our English translations read smoothly. For example, when "Lord" or "God" appear, they might represent any of a number of different Hebrew words. That is why the scriptures presented in this text are literal translations, taken from the One New Man Bible.

The literal translations in this book may not be exactly like any translation of the scriptures you have seen before. Some differences are very significant.

A number of the names are listed more than once, since the different Hebrew and Greek words have nuances that give insight.

Descriptive phrases, such as "The Lord Your God Will Fight For You," may not normally be considered to be "names," but since they do reveal characteristics of God, they are included.

May many of these word studies on the names of God prove to be a blessing to you. If some name does not appeal to you, spark your interest, or quicken your spirit, do not use it – go on to another. However, do hang on to the names that do bear witness to you and use them in your prayers, your teaching, and your conversation. They will help you to develop a deeper relationship with God, enhance your teaching, and enrich other aspects of your life. Do not be put off by anything in this text you do not happen to like; rather, take a firm hold of those you do like.

Ellicott's Commentary on the Whole Bible tells us that God's name is His self-revelation. The name further signifies the active presence of the person in the fullness of the revealed character according to The New Bible Dictionary.

This God we serve desires real relationship with each one of His children. This is a relationship that stretches our imaginations to reach the levels to which He is calling each one of us. As Jesus said in Matthew 12:50, *For whoever would do the will of My Father, the One in the Heavens, this one is My brother and sister and mother.* These studies can help you develop a personal relationship with the most loving Father of all time.

In this study, the Names of God are organized into chapters, with each chapter describing some aspect or function of the Deity.

This book should be viewed as a tool to be used daily in prayer to answer needs, to minister to others as well as deal with personal needs. Whenever we feel abandoned, turning to His Abiding Presence and reading those verses brings a comfort and an assurance, especially when tied to chapters on Love, Refuge, Defender, Power, Authority, and whatever others the Spirit inspires.

The Names in this book are also good source material for Bible studies and sermons. They can be used for emphasis or as the subject of an aspect or function of the Deity. The length of the chapter is not in itself significant. One chapter may contain names that supplement each other and are woven together to bring us to an understanding of a complex theme, while another chapter may emphasize a single use.

Anyone having Hebrew and Greek concordances will enjoy looking up the verses in which the Hebrew or Greek Name is used. One of the Names used for Abiding Presence is found over one hundred fifty times in just the first five books of the Bible! But you must have a Hebrew concordance to find them.

The purpose of this book is to provide you with a better understanding of Who God is. It should inform you and, hopefully, you will find the stimulus for further personal study. If you enjoy digging into Scripture to discover the treasures of deeper meanings, this study should suggest many projects. Keep a pad handy to write the words and Scripture references that especially appeal to you, that quicken your spirit. It will add substance if you use a Hebrew and Greek concordance; which are invaluable tools for finding additional uses of Hebrew and Greek words.

Transliterations, spelling a Hebrew or Greek word in English, are a challenge. They are difficult – awkward at best – because the Hebrew and Greek languages have sounds that do not appear in English. That makes any transliteration awkward.

Both those languages have gutturals, for instance; Americans, especially, have a hard time with these sounds.

All reference numbers given in the text are coded to Strong's Concordance so it is easy to look up those words in the Hebrew and Greek concordances and lexicons that are recommended in Conclusion, which are coded to Strong's numbers. The Strong's number is placed in brackets [ ] in this text immediately after each word being defined.

The verses used here are representative of those in which the various names are found, but they are not necessarily the most powerful ones using a particular name. Quite a few of the verses were chosen, in fact, simply because those were the first verses of the Bible in which the names were found.

Verbs are translated with the traditional English infinitive.

Hebrew root words are given in the currently accepted manner as ts-d-k, with no added vowels. Past practice often used the letter "a" between the root letters, which gives a past tense pronunciation, and sometimes now uses the present tense vowels, which would be tsodek, in this case. So any reader who prefers one of those choices can add the appropriate vowels of his choice.

The Hebrew language has a light guttural sound that is indicated in the transliterations with an "h" or a "kh." The Greek language has a heavier guttural that is indicated by a "ch."

CHAPTER 1

The Godhead

Names Introduced in Chapter 1

God	Elohim
One	Ehad
Only God	Mono Theo
Spirit of God	Ruah Elohim
Lord	LORD*
Lord God	Adonai LORD*
God	El
Image	Eikon

God reveals Himself to us in His Word as He takes us from the very beginning of the world in Genesis to the Eternal Kingdom shown to us in the Prophets and Revelation. Many of these self-revelations of God, these characteristics, teach us about Him and may be written as individual words while others are phrases. Those individual words can rightly be called the Names of God. Whether they are single words or long phrases they open to us a complex, living, loving God Whom, although we do not fully understand Him, we can come to know and love and serve Him.

In the first chapter of Genesis, this God we serve introduces us to His Power.

THIS GOD WE SERVE

God

> *In the beginning GOD created the heavens and the earth.*
> (Genesis 1:1)
> - Elohim [430], God (plural)

This very first name of God in the Bible speaks of judgment and ruling authority. This use of the plural, in fact, is called the majestic plural. It is interesting that Elohim, the plural, uses a singular verb, barah [1254]. The singular verb is important in emphasizing God's unity and His power. When elohim refers to leaders of the people in Genesis 6:2 & 4 it takes a plural verb, as it does in Exodus 32:1 in reference to heathen gods. Barah means to shape or create and is used only in reference to divine activity.

Elohim has the power to create the universe with nothing more than the spoken word! Every word translated God in Genesis 1 is Elohim. Elohim is used over 600 times in reference to God, and is nearly always translated God. It can also be used to refer to false gods and, occasionally, to men, as in Genesis 6:2 & 4. Although often translated sons of gods, in Genesis 6:2 & 4 it is more appropriately expressed as rulers or distinguished men. In Exodus 4:16 Elohim is used to describe Moses as Aaron's 'leader.' The end of that verse is .. *he will be a mouth for you, and you will be his leader.* Another interpretation is that the sons of Elohim were those who worshipped God, while the daughters of men were those who did not worship God, describing unequally yoked marriages.

There were a number of Godly people at that time. *And to Seth, a son was born to him also and he called his name Enosh. Then men began to call upon the name of the LORD*.* (Genesis 4:26)

Elohim is the name of God associated with judgment because that is the name used when God is speaking of judgment.

One
> *Listen! Obey, O Israel! The LORD* is our God! The LORD* is*
> ***ONE!*** (Deuteronomy 6:4)
>> - Ehad [259], one, single, first

The verses in Deuteronomy 6:4-9, 11:13-21, Numbers 15:37-41
are called The Sh'ma, making a prayer that each Jewish person
is to pray each day, declaring that God is One, and making a
total commitment to Him.

Another verse says He is One and His name is One:
> *And the LORD* will be King over all the earth. In that Day the*
> *LORD* will be* ***ONE*** *and His name* ***ONE.*** (Zechariah 14:9)
>> - Ehad [250], one, single, first

Only God
> *Now to the Eternal King, Immortal, Invisible, the* ***ONLY GOD,***
> *be honor and glory forever and ever, amen.* (1 Timothy 1:17)
>> - Mono [3441], only, alone
>> - Theo [2316], God, any deity

This name is here to emphasize His being *the* **ONLY GOD,**
there is none other. Jude, too, uses this expression, in verse 25.
Can God be divided? This chapter is titled Godhead because
the Godhead includes all aspects of the Divine.

Spirit of God
> *And the earth was totally empty, devoid of all life, both animal*
> *and Plant; and darkness was upon the face of the deep. And*
> *the* ***SPIRIT OF GOD*** *hovered, brooded, over the face of the*
> *waters.* (Genesis 1:2)
>> - Ruah [7307], spirit, breath, wind
>> - Elohim [430], God (plural)

God introduces His Spirit in the second verse of the Bible and
emphasizes the free-moving nature of the Holy Spirit.

LORD

*These are the chronicles of the heavens and of the earth when they were created, in the day that the **LORD*** God made the earth and the heavens.* (Genesis 2:4)
- YHVH [3068], the personal name of God, translated LORD*.

This is the Name that speaks of mercy, forgiveness, because this is the name used when mercy is given in Scripture. It is usually read in Hebrew as Adonai, and therefore translated as LORD*. Sometimes it is written as Jehovah, while others pronounce the Name as Yahweh, but there is no J sound in Hebrew and neither is there a W sound, so we are safe from taking His Name in vain when using either Jehovah or Yahweh because neither could be correct. The Name is neither written (except in Scripture) nor spoken by Jewish people out of respect for the Father, and because of the injunction of the third commandment, *You will not take the name of the LORD* your God in vain, for the LORD* will not hold him guiltless who takes His name in vain.* (Exodus 20:7)

Jewish people frequently write or say Hashem, meaning The Name, instead of using FOUR Hebrew letters. We do not call our earthly fathers by their first names, so can we even think of calling our heavenly Father by His? Notice that He introduces the rest of the Godhead first. As God here summarizes His creation it is as though He says, "By the way, I'm your narrator. My name is LORD*."

LORD God

*Then go! Come to those of the captivity, to the children of your people! Speak to them and tell them, whether they will listen or whether they will not listen, Thus says **ADONAI, the LORD***.* (Ezekiel 3:11)
- Adonai [136], lord, commander, ruler, possessor
- LORD* [3068], the personal name of God

"The combined name represents God's love showing itself in justice, meaning that even when He denies or punishes, His underlying purpose is merciful. Since Ezekiel, more than any other, was the prophet of exile, he uses this Name far more than any other prophet." (Rabbi S. R. Hirsch) This combination is used a total of 293 times, from Genesis on, in Scripture and is usually, but not always, translated Lord God. Adonai by itself means "my Lord" and is listed in Chapter 6, Authority.

God (El)

And she called the name of the LORD that spoke to her, "You are **EL**-Ro'i," for she said, "Have I also here looked after Him Who sees me?* (Genesis 16:13)
- El [410], God
- El speaks of power.

Genesis 16:13 is the first use of the singular for God. El can also be used in reference to a false god and can even refer to a man of rank and power.

Image

*And if indeed our gospel has been covered, it has been hidden to the lost, 4. among whom the god of this age blinded the minds of the unbelievers so the light of the Good News of the glory of Messiah, Who is the **IMAGE** of God, did not shine forth. (2 Corinthians 4:3,4)*
- Eikon [1504], image, likeness

Messiah is God Incarnate, the bodily form of the King of the Universe. Savior, Ruler, Mighty, King, King of Kings, Lord, Lord of Lords, Help, Husband, I AM, Judge, Man, and Redeemer are all names that are shared by both Father and Son. It is no wonder that Jesus said, *We the Father and I are **ONE**.* (John 10:30)

God introduces Himself to us as the Godhead, showing us immediately His power to create the universe from nothing! Next the Holy Spirit moves on the face of the waters, and then His spoken Word brings light. Word is also a name for Jesus, with four examples listed in Chapter 3. They are from Psalm

107:20, Revelation 19:13, 1 John 1:1, and John 1:1,14. Only intellectually can we separate God because His characteristics are so intertwined that we have to know He is One. We can assign some of His characteristics to one aspect of His Being, as Jesus is God Incarnate and brought the full power of God to the fore while He was physically on earth.

CHAPTER 2

Holy Spirit

Names Introduced in Chapter 2

Well of the Living One Seeing Me	B'er Lahai Ro'i
Well of the Living One My Seer	B'er Lahai Ro'i
Fountain of Living Waters	Mekor Hayim Mayim
His Eyes	Eniv
Reveals Secrets	Gale Razya
Comforter	Paraklete
One Comforting the Lowly	Parakalon
Spirit of Truth	To Pneuma tes Alethes
Spirit of Grace and Supplications	Ruah Hen Tahenunim
His Eyes	Eniv
Seven Eyes	Shivah Enayim
Seven are the Eyes of the Lord	Shivah-Eleh Ene
Seven Spirits	Ton Hepta Pneumaton
Spirit of Wisdom	Ruah Hakham
Spirit of Understanding	Ruah Vinah
Spirit of Counsel	Ruah Etsah
Spirit of Might	Ruah Gevorah
Spirit of Knowledge	Ruah Da-at
Spirit of Reverence	Ruah Yareh
Spirit of Awe	Ruah Yareh

The Spirit of God has no bounds, no restraints, and is first described to us as moving on the face of the waters (Genesis 1:2). The Spirit of God sees us wherever we are, whatever our condition, whatever our plight. When Hagar ran away from Sarai and Abram, the Angel of the Lord found her in the wilderness by a spring of water and instructed her to return and submit to her mistress. Only the Spirit of God knew where she was – to find her, to minister to her, to prophesy to her regarding her unborn child, and to give her son the name Ishmael.

Well of the Living One Seeing Me

Therefore the well was called "Beer-Lakhai-Ro'I," **WELL OF THE LIVING ONE SEEING ME.** *Behold, it is between Kadesh and Bered.* (Genesis 16:14)
- Be'er [875], well
- La*h*ai [2416], living one
- Ro'i [7210], seeing, looking, sight

Well (Be'er) speaks of a spring, that is living water, a symbol of the Holy Spirit. Living One (Lakhai) is the first record of man referring to God as living. This is Hagar speaking, and while many think of her as not being very spiritual, Hagar knew God. It is no wonder, then, that her prayers were answered. Seeing Me (Ro'i) is the first time the Holy Spirit is referred to as seeing, as acting as the eyes of God. God does indeed see us wherever we are, meeting us in our current circumstances, no matter how desperate.

Well of the Living One My Seer

And Isaac came from the way of the **WELL** *Lahai-Roi,* **OF THE LIVING ONE MY SEER***, for he was living in the south country.* (Genesis 24:62)
- Be'er [875], well
- La*h*ai [2416], living one
- Ro'i [7203], seer, prophet

Another word for prophet, navi is used much more frequently than ro'i but the meanings are basically the same. Several prophets are referred to one time as seer and another as navi.

The word Seer appears frequently, scattered among the books of Scripture, from here (its first use) to Ezra, one of the very last-written books of the Old Testament. The root word of ro'i is r'-ah [7200], meaning to see. (While some scholars believe this should be translated seeing me, the same as in Genesis 16:13, there is strong support for its translation as seer, so seer is included.) We know the Holy Spirit is the agent in every genuinely true prophecy, so it is certainly appropriate. It is interesting that the second use of seer (ro'eh) is in 1 Samuel 9:9, which goes on to say that seer is what prophets used to be called. The difference between ro'eh and ro'i is that the i indicates the personal pronoun my. (In Hebrew, personal pronouns are often suffixes.)

Fountain of Living Waters

Be astonished, O you heavens, at this and be horribly afraid. Be very desolate, says the LORD, 13. for My people have committed two immoral things: they have forsaken Me, the **FOUNTAIN OF LIVING WATERS**, and hewn out cisterns for themselves, broken cisterns that can hold no water.* (Jeremiah 2:12,13)

- Mekor [4726], fountain, spring, source
- Hayim [2416], living
- Mayim [4325], waters

Living Waters are waters that are always flowing, always fresh, thus symbolizing the Holy Spirit. It is interesting that the Artscroll Tanach (OT) translates this as the Source of Living Waters, as surely He is the Source of all life. The following name displays yet another function of the Spirit of God:

Reveals Secrets

*As for you, O king, your thoughts came into your mind upon your bed, what should happen hereafter and He Who **REVEALS SECRETS** makes known to you what will be.* (Daniel 2:29)

- Gale [1541], revealer
- Razya [7328], secrets

These words are Aramaic, but describe the same Holy Spirit that gave the prophecy to Hagar. The following name likewise presents a functional character of the Holy Spirit.

Comforter

*If you love Me, you will keep My commandments: 16. and I will ask the Father and, so that He would be with you forever, He will give you another **COMFORTER**,* (John 14:15,16)

*But the **COMFORTER**, the Holy Spirit which the Father will send in My name, that One will teach you all things and remind you of all which I told you.* (John 14:26)

*But I Myself tell you the truth. It is profitable for you that I should go. For if I do not go away, the **COMFORTER** will not come to you."* (John 16:7)
- Paraklete [3875], called to one's side, intercessor, mediator, comforter, advocate

Paraklete is also used once to refer to Jesus, *My little children, I write these things to you so that you would not sin. But if anyone does sin, we have an **Advocate** with the Father, Jesus Messiah, the righteous:*

(1 John 2:1)
This time it is translated advocate, and explains Jesus' statement in John 14:16 that the Father will send another Comforter. Both the Holy Spirit and Jesus intercede for us and encourage us.

The One Comforting the Lowly

*For indeed (on) our (Paul and Timothy) coming into Macedonia our flesh has had no rest, but in every way being troubled; (with) fightings on the outside, fears within. But **THE ONE COMFORTING THE LOWLY** comforted us.* (2 Corinthians 7:5,6)

- Ho Parakale [3870], to call to one's side, to console, to encourage, to comfort Tous Tapeinous [5011], not far from the ground, of low degree, brought low with grief, depressed

We should certainly be encouraged, knowing that when there are strivings on the outside, depression or fears within, the same Holy Spirit who comforted Paul and Timothy is eager to bring us His comfort.

The Spirit of Truth

THE SPIRIT OF TRUTH, Whom the world is not able to accept, because it does not see and does not know Him: you know Him, because He remains beside you and will be inside you. (John 14:17)
- To Pneuma [4151], spirit, wind
- Tes Aletheias [225], truth

Jesus is speaking of the Holy Spirit, as He did in Acts 1:8, you will receive power when the Holy Spirit comes upon you.

Spirit of Grace and Supplications

And I shall pour the **SPIRIT OF GRACE AND SUPPLICATIONS** *upon the house of David and upon the inhabitants of Jerusalem, and they will look to Me Whom they have pierced (John 19:37) and they will mourn for Him, as one mourns for his only son and will be in bitterness for Him, as one that is in bitterness for his firstborn.* (Zechariah 12:10)
- Ruah [7307], spirit
- Hen [2580], grace, favor
- Tahenoonim [8469], supplications for favor

Both Hen and Tahenoonim come from the same root, h-n-n [2603], meaning to show favor, to be gracious.

This name shows the Holy Spirit as our intercessor, making supplication in our behalf for the Father to show us favor and to be gracious to us.

His Eyes

*For the **EYES** of the LORD* run to and fro throughout the whole earth, to show Himself strong on behalf of those who look toward Him with their whole heart. Here you have done foolishly, therefore from now on you will have wars.* (2 Chronicles 16:9)
- Eniv [5869], his eyes

This was spoken by Hanani the prophet to Asa, to remind Asa that he was wrong to call on the king of Syria for help in fighting the enemies of Judah. Even so for us, our first reaction often is to deal with our problems in the flesh – ignoring the fact that the Eyes of the Lord are with us. God's desire, if only we will let Him, is to show us His strength. We tie His hands when we reason things out and move ahead with our own plans and alliances.

Seven Eyes

*For behold the stone that I have laid before Joshua, upon one stone will be **SEVEN EYES**. Behold, I shall engrave the engraving, says the LORD* of Hosts, and I shall remove the iniquity of that land in one day.* (Zechariah 3:9)

Seven Are The Eyes

Moreover the word of the LORD came to me saying, 9. The hands of Zerubbabel have laid the foundation of this House. His hands will also finish it and you will know that the LORD* of Hosts has sent me to you. 10. For who has despised the day of small things?! For they will rejoice and will see the plumb line stone in the hand of Zerubbabel with those **SEVEN**. (Isa. 11:2) They **ARE the EYES** of the LORD*, which run to and fro through the whole earth.* (Zechariah 4:8-10)
- Shivah [7651], seven
- Enayim [5869], eyes

Seven Spirits

John to the seven churches that are in Asia: Grace to you and peace from the One Who is, and Who Was, and the One Who Is

12

*Coming and from the **SEVEN SPIRITS** which are before His throne.* (Revelation 1:4)

And you must write to the messenger of the congregation in Sardis:

*The One Who has the **SEVEN SPIRITS** of God and the seven stars says these things: I know your deeds and that you have a reputation, that of life, but you are dead.* (Revelation 3:1)

*And lightnings and voices and thunders were going out from the throne, and in front of the throne seven lamps of fire were burning, which are the **SEVEN SPIRITS** of God,* (Revelation 4:5)

*.. And I also saw in the midst of the throne the four living creatures and in the midst of the elders a Lamb standing as having been slain, having seven horns and seven eyes which are the **SEVEN SPIRITS** of God that were sent into all the earth.* (Revelation 5:6)
- Hepta [2033], seven
- Pneumata [4151], spirit, wind, breath

Why did the Lord have Zechariah and John use the number seven in reference to the Holy Spirit? We know that seven is the number of completion (perfection), which is certainly appropriate for the Spirit of God.

The seven-fold character of the Holy Spirit is spelled out in Isaiah 11:2 and can be enumerated as below.

1. The Spirit of Wisdom and
2. Understanding
3. The Spirit of Counsel and
4. Might
5. The Spirit of Knowledge and
6. Reverence and
7. Awe

And there will come forth a shoot out of the trunk of Jesse, and a Branch will grow out of his roots: 2. and the Spirit of the LORD* will rest upon Him, the Spirit of 1 WISDOM and 2 UNDERSTANDING, the Spirit of 3 COUNSEL and 4 MIGHT, the Spirit of 5 KNOWLEDGE and of the 6 REVERENCE and 7 AWE of the LORD*. (Isaiah 11:1,2)
- Ruah [7307], spirit, breath, wind
- Hakhmah [2451], wisdom
- Vinah [998], understanding
- Etsah [6098], counsel, advice
- Gevurah [1369], mighty, strong, valiant
- Da-at [1847], knowledge
- Yir-at [3373], revere

Examine each characteristic of the seven-fold Holy Spirit:

1. Wisdom-
Not from man's intellect, but straight from the Throne Room,
Happy is the man who finds wisdom and the man who gets understanding. 14. For its merchandise is better than the merchandise of silver and its increase than fine gold. 15. It is more precious than pearls and all the things you compared to it. 16. Length of days is in its right hand; in its left hand riches and honor. 17. Its ways are ways of pleasantness and all its paths are peace. 18. It is a tree of life to those who lay hold on it and happy is everyone who retains it. 19. The LORD by **wisdom** has founded the earth; by understanding He has established the heavens.* (Proverbs 3:13-19)

*He has made the earth by His power. He has established the world by His **wisdom** and has stretched out the heavens at His discretion.* (Jeremiah 10:12)

Who is wise and learned among you? He must constantly show by good conduct his works of wisdom in humility. 14. But if you have bitter jealousy and strife in your heart, do not boast against and do not tell lies against the truth. 15. This wisdom is not wisdom coming down from above, but is earthly, worldly, proceeding from an evil spirit. 16. For where there is jealousy *and strife, from that place is disorder and every worthless, wicked deed. 17. But the **wisdom** from above is indeed first pure, then peaceable, kind, obedient, full of mercy and of good fruits, unwavering, without hypocrisy. 18. And the fruit of acts of loving kindness is sown in peace by those who make peace.* (Jacob 3:13-18) (See also Jeremiah 51:15, Psalm 104:24, Proverbs 8:1-36, and 9:1).

God's Wisdom is not our rationalizing, but His Spirit bringing us His Wisdom. His ways are not our ways, so we should not rely on our own reasonings (common sense) but, in prayer, rely on His Spirit. As Paul wrote,
O Timothy, you must now guard the deposit, turning away for yourself from the profane chatter and contradictions of what is falsely called knowledge, (1 Timothy 6:20)

2. Understanding-
The Hebrew root, b-i-n [995] means to discern.
You will guide me with Your counsel and afterward take me to glory.

This is the same as the gift of discernment in 1 Corinthians 12:10. The gift of understanding is the gift of discernment. In Proverbs 8:14b God says *I am Understanding.*

3. Counsel-
*You will guide me with Your **counsel** and afterward take me to glory.*
(Psalm 73:24)
***Counsel** and sound Wisdom are mine:* (Proverbs 8:14a)
Also this comes forth from the LORD of Hosts, doing wonders in **Counsel**, making sound Wisdom great.* (Isaiah 28:29)
*There is no wisdom and no understanding and **no counsel** against the LORD*.* (Proverbs 21:30)

Surely God is telling us to stop storing up our knowledge of men, even Godly men. And He tells each one of us to rely more and more on the Holy Spirit to bring us God's Wisdom, Understanding, and Advice. This means spending hours in His

Word, in prayer, in fasting, and in total obedience. Sensitivity to the counsel of the Holy Spirit cannot be gained by studying this book or any other book written by man. It can be acquired only by careful obedience in doing the will of the Father.

Not everyone who says to Me, 'Lord. Lord!' will enter the kingdom of the heavens, but the one who does the will of My Father, the One in the heavens. (Matthew 7:21) See also verses 22-29.

4. Might-

*Listen, you who are far off, to what I have done! And, you who are near, acknowledge My **might**! Selah.* (Isaiah 33:13)

God's Power is extended to us by His Spirit.

This is the same Power that enabled His Word to create the earth and about which Jesus spoke:
..whoever would say to this mountain, 'You must immediately be removed and you must immediately be cast into the sea,' and would not doubt in his heart but would believe that what he is saying is happening, it shall be to him. (Mark 11:23)

Since there is no one like You, LORD, Your name is Great and Your name is Great in **MIGHT**.* (Jeremiah 10:6)

The Spirit of Might, therefore, is now available to us, to move mountains, to heal, to do spiritual warfare.

These four aspects of the Holy Spirit are to be received by us: Wisdom, understanding (Discernment), Counsel, and Might. They are gifts from God, but they must be taken by faith. The remaining three aspects of the Seven-fold Spirit require something from us.

5. Knowledge-

*Teach me good judgment and **KNOWLEDGE**, for I have believed Your commandments. 67. Before I was afflicted I went astray, but now I have kept Your word.* (Psalm 119:64-66)

My son, if you will take my words and hide my commandments with you, 2. so that you incline your ear to wisdom, applying your heart to understanding, 3. and if you cry after intelligence and lift up your voice for understanding, 4. if you seek it as silver and search for it as for hidden treasures, 5. then you will understand the reverence of the LORD and find the **KNOWLEDGE** of God.* (Proverbs 2:1-5)

And all your children will be taught by the LORD*, and the peace of your children will be great. (Isaiah 54:13)

(Jesus speaking) *It has been written in the Prophets, 'And all will be taught by God:' (Isa. 54:13) everyone who has heard and learned from the Father comes to Me.* (John 6:45)

At that time Y'shua said, "I praise You, Father, Master of Heaven and Earth, because You hid these things from the wise and intelligent and You revealed them to babies: (Matthew 11:25)

Just as Jesus chose disciples who worked with their hands, and did not choose scribes, we must come to Him with open hearts. We cannot strengthen our knowledge of God with our intellectual exercises alone, but by being open and letting His Spirit teach us. Jesus said:
My teaching is not Mine, but of the One Who sent Me: (John 7:16)

Then His Spirit can teach us all things. If we fail to put His Word in ourselves, then His Spirit will have nothing with which to work and will not be able to teach us. If we hunger and thirst after His righteousness, spending extended time every day in the Word, then the Holy Spirit will have the raw materials with which to work. Only then can He teach us.

In Jesus' day education was mandatory for Jewish boys. Jewish girls could be excused if their help was needed at home. School consisted of learning Scripture; each synagogue having its own school. The children started memorizing Scripture by the age of five (pre-school), beginning with the book of Leviticus, the book of holiness. By the age of twelve they had committed the entire Torah (the first five books of the Bible) to memory. Scrolls were very expensive, so only the wealthy had personal copies of the Torah, Prophets, and Writings, the Old Testament. However, many had memorized all Hebrew Scripture, plus Midrash (Study).

Reading the sermons of Peter, Stephen, and Paul in the Book of Acts should convince us of how well grounded the disciples were. In gaining knowledge, our first responsibility is to put the Word in us. Only then can the Spirit teach us all things. Knowledge, then, might be thought of as the interface characteristic of the Holy Spirit, with action going both ways. But we need to study so the Holy Spirit can teach us the deep meanings of Scripture.

6. Reverence

REVERENCE for the LORD* is the beginning of wisdom: a good understanding have all those who do His commandments. His praise endures forever. (Psalm 111:10)

23:3. The God of Israel said, the Rock of Israel spoke to me, He who rules over men must be just, ruling in reverence of God. 4. And he will be like the light of the morning, when the sun rises, a morning without clouds, like the tender grass springing out of the earth by shining clear after rain. (2 Samuel 23:3, 4)

Jesus is ruling in obedience. David speaks here of Messiah and we know that Jesus is our ultimate example of obedience to God's perfect will in every step He walked and every word

He spoke. He is also the paragon of reverence. Of these two qualities, reverence and obedience, obedience seems to be the more troublesome. We can be disobedient, even by trying to do good things, if we don't first seek Him. How many of us could respond day in and day out as Jesus did? At the pool called Bethesda were a great number (possibly hundreds) of infirm, blind, lame, withered, all awaiting the stirring of the water. All of them were believers in the Living God and each was there hoping for God to bring healing. My fleshly impulse in that situation would be to lay hands on each one, to pray for healing. Jesus, however, singled out just one man and asked him one brief question, *"Do you desire to become whole?"* The answer to that question was in the man's heart, although not in his open response, which was that he had no one to cast him into the pool. Jesus' healing statement was, *"Rise, take up your mattress and walk."* (John 5:2-9) There is no record of Jesus' having spoken to or having healed anyone else there. Also, just as it is possible to be reverent without obedience, we can be obedient without being wholly reverent.

7. Awe –

Do not be in AWE, Abram! I AM your Shield! Your reward will be exceedingly great. (Genesis 15:1)

Numbers, Chapters 22 through 24 tell of Balaam being asked by Balak to curse Israel. Balaam would not go with Balak's representatives without God's approval. But Balaam would not take "No" for an answer, so he went in God's permissive will. After he arrived in Moab he spoke only what God gave him. *But Balaam answered and said to Balak, "Did I not I tell you, saying, All that the LORD* speaks, that I must do?"* (Numbers 23:26)

And Balaam said to Balak, "Did I not also tell your messengers whom you sent to me saying, 13. 'If Balak would give me his house full of silver and gold, I cannot go beyond the commandment of the LORD*, to do good or bad of my own mind, but what the LORD* says, that will I speak?'" (Numbers 24:12,13)

Balaam was careful to be obedient, but earlier had talked to God like a child pleading for permission to do something after a parent says "No." *And God said to Balaam, "You will not go with them! You will not curse the people, for they are blessed."* (Numbers 22:12)

God was certainly clear: *"You will not go."* But Balaam, like a child, did not respect this answer, having to plead for permission to go. Right at the beginning of his meeting with Balak, Balaam said, *"Come, I shall advise you.."* Balaam was obedient to the extent that he prophesied a true word to Balak, but, since his advice apparently led to the harlotry of Numbers 25:1, he paid for his treachery with his life (Numbers 31:8). When Israel killed the kings of Midian, Balaam was added to the list. The story clearly warns us that we have to be both reverent and in awe of the Living God. Balaam did not hold God in Awe.

The Hebrew word Yar-e has by tradition been translated Fear, but that tradition is because the first English translations were made from Latin, with the Latin text having Timeo which does mean fear. Those who revere God and serve Him are not to fear or even be Awed by their spiritual, physical, or emotional enemies.

Fear is not an option for believers. Do not even be awed by your obstacles. Have faith that He is on your side and will fight for you.

There is no place in the Hebrew scriptures saying to Fear God. Fear would be a hindrance to our relationship with Him, the most Loving Father ever. Pahad is the Hebrew word for fear and it is used as Fear of God only for heathens and backsliders, never for Godly people.

The Seven-fold Holy Spirit presents the Holy Spirit as the Great Communicator, and as the agent through Whom God makes His Power available to men. Since Elohim spoke to create things we know that God can do anything He wants and does not need people. Throughout history, though, we see the Lord working through people, or even a donkey (Numbers 22:21-31), and people do not do wondrous works unless the Holy Spirit has come upon them. Anyone who desires the Holy Spirit to work through him (or her) must reach a state of total commitment to God. Jesus did not move in ministry (power) until after His baptism in the Holy Spirit. He said, *"We, the Father and I, are One."* (John 10:20) God can at His pleasure work through unbelievers as He did with Cyrus (Ezra 1:1,2), but those who are seeking to move in the power of the Holy Spirit need to follow the example of Jesus. The Holy Spirit functions as the Eyes and Ears (carrying our supplications) of the Lord. The Holy Spirit knows no bounds on earth or in the heavens, but roams even more freely than the wind, which, unlike Him, is limited to the earth's atmosphere. The Holy Spirit is the Great Communicator, bringing us wisdom, understanding, and revealing the truths hidden in God's Word. He brings the prophetic according to Joel 2:28 *And I will pour out My Spirit on all flesh and your sons and your daughters will prophesy.* His purpose is to encourage and comfort and to bring power. How blessed we are to have God's Spirit upon us. To receive these blessings of the Spirit-filled life, we must be rooted in the Word, then totally committed to God: nothing less than 100% commitment. Our commitment is expressed in reverential and obedient fear of the Lord.

The Seven-fold Holy Spirit gives us the Gifts of the Spirit:
And there are varieties of gifts, but the same Spirit: 5. and there are varieties of ministry, but the same Lord: 6. and there are varieties of activities, but the same God, the One Who works all things in all people. 7. And to each is given the manifestation of the Spirit toward that which is profitable for all. 8. For indeed through the Spirit to one is given a word of wisdom, and to another a word of knowledge according to the same Spirit, 9. to another faith by the same Spirit, and to another gifts of healings by the one Spirit, 10. and to another activities that call forth miracles, and to another prophecy, and to another discernings of spirits (John 16:8), to another to speak in different kinds of tongues, and to another interpretation of tongues: 11. But the one and the same Spirit operates all these things, distributing His own gifts to each, just as He wishes. (1 Corinthians 12:4-11)

These verses from 1 Corinthians not only show us what the gifts are, but that they are given to us for good use, for "God's purposes." They are not given to us for entertainment or so that we may enjoy Holy Ghost goose bumps. They are given to bring healing, comfort, deliverance, and all of God's provisions and power to the Body of Messiah.

CHAPTER 3

Messiah

Names Introduced in Chapter 3

Shiloh	Shiloh
Name	Onomati
Salvation	Yeshuatkha
Help	Lishua
Victories	Yeshu-ot
Welfare	Yeshuati
Health	Yeshu-ot
Saving Health	Yeshuate-kha
Deliverance	Yeshu-ot
Jesus	Iesous
Hosanna	Hosanna
Mighty One of Jacob	Avir Yaakov
Shepherd	Ro-eh
The Good Shepherd	Ho Poiman ho Kalos
The Great Shepherd	Ton Poimena ton Megan
Chief Shepherd	Archipoimenos
Stone of Israel	Ehven Yisrael
My Redeemer	Go-ali
Angel Who Redeemed Me	HaMale-kha HaGo-el
Redeemer	Go-el
Angel of His Presence	Male-akh Panaiv
Word	Devar

The Word	Ho Logos
Word of Life	Tou Logou tes Zoes
The Word of God	Ho Logos Tou Theos
Miracle	Peli
Wonder	Peli
Bread of the Presence	Lehem haPanim
Living Bread Ho	Artos ho Zon
Lamp	Ner
Light	Or
The Light	Ton Photos
Daystar	Phosphoros
The First and the Last	Ho Protos kai ho Eschatos
The Living One	Ho Zon
The Head	He Kephale
Beginning	Arche
Firstborn Out From the Dead	Prototokos ek tov Nekron
First	Proteuov
Alef and Tav	Alpha and Omega
Lord of Hosts	Ho Pantokrator
The Almighty	Ho Pantokrator
Beginning and the End	Alef and Tav
First and Last	Rishon ve-et Ahronim
Amen	Amen
The Faithful and True Witness	Ho Martus ho Pistos kai, Alethinos
The Head	He Arche
Heir	Kleronomon
The Ruler of the	Ho Archon ton
Kings of the Earth	Basileon tes Ges
Lord of Lords	Kurios Kurion
King of Kings	Basileus Basileon
Head of Every Principality and	He Kephale Pases Arches, Kai Eksousias

One Ruling	Moshel
Judge	Krites
The Lord of Glory	Ton Kurion tes Dokses
The Bridegroom	Ho Numphios
God is With Us	Imanu El
I Am With You	Ego Meth Hemon
I AM	Ego Eimi
Husband	Ish
Captain of the Host	Sar Tseva
Wonder	Pele
Counselor	Yo-ets
Mighty God	El Gibor
Everlasting Father	Avi Ad
Prince of Peace	Sar Shalom
Shoot	Hoter
Branch	Netser
Your Right Hand	Yemine-kha
Man of Your Right Hand	Ish Yemine-kha
Son of Man	Ben Adam
Son of Man	Kevar Enash
Root of Jesse	Shoresh Yishai
My Servant	Avdi
My Elect	Behiri
My Shepherd	Ro-i
Man	Gever
My Associate	Amiti
Hope of Israel	Mikveh Israel
Savior	Moshi-o
The Hope of Israel	Tes Elpidos tou Israel
Righteous Sprout	Tsemah Tsadik
Lord Our Righteousness	Tsidkenu
The Just One	Tou Dikai-ou

Upright One	Yashar
Sun of Acts of Loving Kindness	Shemesh Tsedakah
Stone	Aven
Tried Stone	Ehven Bohen
Precious Cornerstone	Pinat Yikrat
Cornerstone	Akrogoviaion
Main Cornerstone	Kephalen Gonias
Sure Foundation	Musad Musad
The Stone Ho	Lithos
Stone of Stumbling	Aven Negef
Rock of Falling	Tsur Mihshol
Stone of Stumbling	Lithon Proskommatos
Rock of Offense	Petran Skandalou
Your King	Malkekh
Humble	Ani
The King of the Jews	Ho Basileus ton Ioudaion
The Coming One	Ho Erchomenos
The Messiah	Ho Christos
The King of Israel	Ho Basileus Israel
Lord of All	Panton Kurios
The Messiah	Ho Christos
Messiah	Christos
The Mashiakh	Ton Messian
Mashiakh Prince	Mashiah Nagid
My Messiah	Mashihi
Brings Good News	Mevaser
The Lion out of the Tribe of Judah	Ho Leon ho ek Fules Iouda
The Root of David	He Riza Dauid
The Lamb	Ho Amnos
Lamb	Arnion
The Firstborn	Ton Prototokon

Son of David	Huiou Dauid
Son of Abraham	Huiou Abraham
Son of David	Huios Dauid
The Bright and	Ho Aster ho lampos
Morning Star	Ho Proinos
My Son	Ton Huion Mou
My Son	Veni
The Son of the	Ho Huios tou Theou
Living God	Tou Zontos
Son of the Most High	Huios Hupsistou
Lord of the Harvest	Tou Kurion tou Therismou
The Son of Man	Ho Huios tou Anthropou
Lord of the Sabbath	Kurios tou Sabbatou
The Master Ton	Despoten
Master	Epistata
Dayspring	Anatole
Comforter of Israel	Paraklesin tou Israel
The Teacher	Ton Didaskalon
The Passover	To Pascha Humon
The Bread of Life	Ho Artos tes Zoes
The Door	He Thura
The Way	He Hodos
The Truth	He Aletheia
The Life	He Zoe
The Resurrection and the Life	He Anastasis kai he Zo
The Author of Life	Ton Archegon tes Zoes
Guarantee	Engus
That Prophet	Tou Prophetou Ekeinou
The Spirit of Prophecy	To Pneuma tes Propheteias
Seed	Sperma
The Seed	To Spermati
Savior	Sotera

Mediator	Mesites
Advocate	Paraklete
The Apostle	Ton Apostolon
Minister	Leitourgos
Priest	Kohen
Forerunner	Prodromos
High Priest	Archiera
Author and Finisher of Our Faith	Archegon kai Teleioten
The Faithful Witness	Ho Martus ho Pistos
Propitiation	Hilasmos
Pious One, Your	Hasidyekha

The Son of God is referred to by many different names. That is obvious by just a glance at the list of names above. Roughly half of those are in Hebrew, an indication of how He is present in references woven throughout all Scripture. The Messiah is first introduced in Jacob's prayer in the 49th chapter of Genesis. This prayer gives us five names including His personal name, Yeshua.

Shiloh
*The scepter will not depart from Judah, nor a Torah scholar from between his feet, until **SHILOH** comes: and the gathering of the peoples will be to Him.* (Genesis 49:10)
- Shiloh [7886], he whose it is, the one men try to reach, messiah

Verses 11 and 12 describe Messiah in greater detail.
Binding His foal to the vine and His donkey's colt to the choice vine, He washed His garments in wine and His clothes in the blood of grapes. 12. His eyes will be red with wine, and His teeth white with milk. (Genesis 49:11,12)

Here Jacob is speaking of Jesus, 1700 years before His birth. This is the only use of Shiloh in Scripture. The root word for shiloh is sh-l-v [7951&7952], meaning to be quiet, at ease, to prosper.

Name

*(The High Priest asked them) saying, Did we not command you not to teach on this **NAME**? And behold you (Peter and John) have filled Jerusalem with your teaching and purpose to bring on us the blood of this Man.* (Acts 5:28)
- Onomati [3686], name

What is this Name? It is the given name of our Lord and Savior, called out by Jacob in his prophetic prayer, extremely rich as we see below.

Yeshuatkha – Your Salvation

*I have waited for **YOUR SALVATION**, LORD**. (Genesis 49:18)
- Yeshuatkha [3444], your deliverance, salvation

The word translated "Salvation" is the feminine form of the personal name of our Lord, **Yeshua**. The feminine form, Yeshuah, is used about seventy-five times in the Hebrew scriptures, and is translated six different ways in the KJV, with similar variations in other translations. The pronoun "your" is in caps along with "salvation," because it is a suffix in Hebrew, attached to Yeshua.

Other translations of Yeshua are given here:

*And he said if the Syrians are stronger than I, then you shall be for me: and if the sons of Ammon are stronger than you, then I will come to **HELP** you.* (2 Samuel 10:11 KJV)
- Lishuah [3444], help

*He gave His king great **VICTORIES**; He shows unfailing kindness to His anointed, to David and his descendants forever.* (2 Samuel 22:51 NIV)
- Yeshu-ot [3444], victories

*Terrors are turned upon me: they pursue my soul as the wind: and my **WELFARE** passeth away as a cloud.* (Job 30:15 KJV)
   - Yeshuati [3444], welfare

*Why are thou cast down, O my soul? and art thou disquieted within me? hope in God; for I shall yet praise Him, Who is the **HEALTH** of my countenance, and my God.* (Psalm 43:5 KJV)
   - Yeshu-ot [3444], health

*That Thy Way may be known upon earth, Thy **SAVING HEALTH** among all nations.* (Psalm 67:2 KJV)
   - Yeshuate-kha [3444], your saving health

*We have been with child, we have been in pain, we have brought forth wind; we have not wrought any **DELIVERANCE** in the earth; neither have the inhabitants of the world fallen.* (Isaiah 26:18 KJV)
   - Yeshu-ot [3444], deliverance

*..and Jacob begat Joseph, the husband of Mary, of whom was born **JESUS**, the One called Messiah."* (Matthew 1:16 KJV)

Iesous (2424), Iesous is not a Greek word, but the spelling of Yeshua (Hebrew) in Greek.

*And the crowds going before Him and those who were following were crying out saying, '**HOSHEA-NA** Son of David: Blessed be the One Who comes in the name of the Lord: **HOSHEA-NA** in the highest.'*
(Ps 118:25,26, from Matthew 21:9)

Hosanna (5614), Hoshea-na or Yeshuana in Hebrew

Yeshua-na is the source of all these qualities:

Victories, Welfare, Health, Saving Health, Deliverance, Jesus, Hosanna: all are translations (of Hebrew) or trans-literations (in New Testament) of the Hebrew word Yeshua. The root of yeshuah, y-sh-a [3467] means to deliver, to save, to be victorious. Yeshuah has been translated most frequently as salvation by Christian translators and deliverance by Jewish translators. The word "Hosanna" is a transliteration into the Greek. The "na" suffix is a polite but demanding "Please! Do!" So Hosanna is demanding "salvation" or "deliverance" now! In the Alcalay Complete Hebrew-English Dictionary, 1990 Edition, the meaning of yeshuah is given as: salvation, help, rescue, prosperity. His name is all those and more.

Now we return to Jacob's prayer in Genesis 49.

Mighty One of Jacob, Shepherd, Stone of Israel

*But his bow abode in strength and the arms of his hands were made strong by the hands of the **MIGHTY ONE OF JACOB**; from there he became the **SHEPHERD**, the **STONE** of **ISRAEL**:* (Genesis 49:24)

- Avir [47], mighty, valiant
- Yaakov [3290], one closely following
- Ro-eh [7462], shepherd
- Ehven [68], stone, here as sacred pillar
- Yisrael [3478], Israel, God persists, perseveres,

It is awesome that Jacob's prayer was so prophetic, that it gives us five names of Jesus, including His personal name. He emphasized the parameters of Jesus' ministry, from Shiloh to Mighty to Shepherd to Rock; Messiah and Power (strength, authority), along with the gentle nurturing and love of the Shepherd; and finally the sacred Foundation Stone. All these are in addition to the meanings of Yeshua, the richest word in this study. Several root words are worth studying. The root of Yaakov is a-k-v [6117] meaning to follow at the heel, to succeed, to bring consequence on, to punish, to make to follow, i.e. to reward or punish. Jacob had a hunger and desire for the things of God that caused him to wrestle all night for a blessing. (Would that we all had that drive to succeed for the things of the Lord.) No wonder God, speaking through Malachi said, *"Yet I loved Jacob. . and Esau I have hated."* (Malachi 1:2,3) The root of

Ro-eh is r'-ah [7462], meaning to pasture, to tend, to graze, and when used with people, to teach. This introduces in Genesis one of the prime functions of the pastor – teaching. Teaching is an integral part for every pastor's work, required to perfect the saints. Many scholars stress that the ministries listed in Ephesians 4:11 total only four, the office of Pastor-Teacher as a single part of a four-fold ministry, instead of two parts of a five-fold. Ehven is used in allusions to Messiah as "Foundation," "Tried Stone," and "Stone of Stumbling." ("Rock" is discussed in Chapter Ten). The Hebrew, Ehven, is the word used for stones that are cut. The root of Ehven is b-n-h [1129], meaning to build. Ehven is used in Isaiah 28:16 with the "Tried Stone," referring to the Stone that was tested and proved acceptable, then rejected by the builders. The rabbis say that God does not literally hate Esau, but this means that He loves Esau less than Jacob. The same expression is used in Genesis 29:31 with Leah and Deuteronomy 21:15 in speaking of two wives. God is Love.

The root of Yisrael, s-r-h [8280] means to persist, to exert oneself, to persevere. This is speaking of Jacob's successful struggle with the agent of God. (Genesis 32:29).

The Good Shepherd
I Myself am **THE GOOD SHEPHERD. THE GOOD SHEPHERD** *lays down His life for the sheep.* (John 10:11)
   - Ho Poimen [4166], the shepherd
   - Ho Kalos [2570], the good

The use of the article with both shepherd and good emphasizes that there is only one Good Shepherd.

The Great Shepherd
Now the God of peace, the One having **THE GREAT SHEPHERD** *of the sheep up out of the dead, in the blood of an eternal covenant, our Lord Jesus.* (Hebrews 13:20)
   - Ton Poimena [4166], shepherd, the presiding officer, manager, director of any assembly, pastor
   - Ton Megan [3173], great, eminent for ability, virtue, authority, power

The name in the next verse, like that in the following speaks of Messiah as Head of the Church, of the Body of Messiah.

The Chief Shepherd

*And when **THE CHIEF SHEPHERD** appears you will receive the unfading crown of glory.* (1 Peter 5:4)
- Tou Archipoimenos [750], Chief Shepherd, of Messiah as Head of the church

This is the only time the word Archipoimenos appears in Scripture. He must not only be Director of the Church, but He must also be Lord of the life of each member of the Body of Messiah.

My Redeemer

*For I know that **MY REDEEMER** lives and that He will stand at the latter day upon the earth,* (Job 19:25)
- Ga-ali [1350], my redeemer

My personal Redeemer is automatically my kinsman Redeemer. The only redeemer in the Hebrew Scriptures is the kinsman. Sometimes in this passage ga-ali is translated Savior.

Angel Who Redeemed Me

*The **ANGEL WHO REDEEMED ME** from everything bad, bless the lads and let my name be named on them, and the name of my fathers Abraham and Isaac and let them grow into a multitude in the midst of the earth."* (Genesis 48:16)
- HaMale-akh [4397], the angel, the messenger
- HaGo-el [1350], the redeemer

This name appears in Jacob's prayer and blessing on Ephraim and Manasseh. The use of the article again emphasizes that there is only one Angel that Redeemed me. Jesus is the only heavenly being with the authority to redeem. Go-el is also translated as Savior.

Redeemer

*And He, Y'shua, will come as **REDEEMER** to Zion and to those who turn from rebellious sin in Jacob, says the LORD*.* (Isaiah 59:20)
- Go-el [1350], redeemer

This name identifies the Lord as a personal (my, your, their) Redeemer. It appears in three Psalms (19:14, 78:35, 103:4), in Proverbs 23:11, thirteen times in Isaiah, and in Jeremiah 50:34. This personal relationship is an inherent character of the Redeemer since the only "redeemer" in Hebrew is the kinsman redeemer. Our kinship, to be in "sonship" to the Father, is an essential part of our redemption. The book of Ruth puts this Hebrew notion of the kinsman redeemer in a clearer perspective.

Angel of His Presence

*In all their affliction He was afflicted, and the **ANGEL OF HIS PRESENCE** saved them: in His love and in His compassion He redeemed them and He bore them, and carried them all the days of old.* (Isaiah 63:9)
- Male-akh [4397], messenger, angel
- Panaiv [6440], his presence

Panaiv literally means "his face." This Hebrew idiom is used very frequently to indicate the presence of God. (See Chapter 12.)

Word

*He will send His **WORD** and He will heal them, and He will deliver them from their demon of destructions.* (Psalm 107:20)
- Devaro [1697], his word

This is the same Word that John spoke of:

The Word

*In the beginning was **THE WORD** and **THE WORD** was with God and God was **THE WORD**.* (John 1:1)
- Tou Logou [3056], the word

The Word of Life

What was from (the) beginning, what we had heard, what we had seen With our eyes, what we had beheld, and our hands had touched, concerning The WORD OF LIFE. (1 John 1:1)
- Ho Logos [3056], the word
- Tes Zoes [2198], of the life

The Word of God

Then I saw heaven opened, and there was a white horse and the One Who sits on it, called Faithful and True, and He judges in righteousness and He makes war. 12. And His eyes are like a flame of fire, and upon His head many crowns. He has a name written which no one knows except Himself, 13. and is clothed in a garment dyed in blood, and His name has been called THE WORD OF GOD. (Revelation 19:11-13)
- Ho Logos [3056], the word
- Tou The-ou [2316], of the God

He was with God in the beginning and that same Word lives with us today, to heal us, to bring life to those who serve Him, to set us free from fears, doubts, and all the concerns of this life.

Miracle

And the angel of the LORD* said to him, Why do you ask this about my name, seeing it is MIRACLE? (Judges 13:18)
- Peli [6383], Wonderful, Miraculous, Amazing, Marvelous, Astounding.

You have beset me behind and before and laid Your hand upon me. 6. Such knowledge is too WONDERFUL for me: it is high, I cannot attain to it. (Psalm 139:5,6)
- Peli-aih [6383], wonderful, incomprehensible

The root of Peli and Peli-aih is p-l-a [6381], meaning to be surpassing, to be extraordinary. What fitting descriptions for the Son! These are the only two uses of this word in the Hebrew Canon.

Bread of the Presence

*And Solomon made all the vessels for the House of God, the golden altar also, and the tables on which the **BREAD OF THE PRESENCE** was set.* (2 Chronicles 4:19)
- Lehem [3899], bread, food in general
- HaPanim [6440], the presence, face

The Bread of the Presence is also called the Showbread. It was placed on the table of the tabernacle, and also (as in this reference) in the Temple, after it had been built. Bread represents Jesus; Bread of the Presence speaks of Him in the presence of the Father. Wherever you see "Showbread," it is a translation of "Lehem HaPanim," and literally means "Bread of the Presence."

The Living Bread

*I AM **THE LIVING BREAD** that descended from out of heaven: if anyone would eat of this Bread he will live forever, and also the Bread which I will give on behalf of the life of the world is My flesh.* (John 6:51)
- Ho Artos [740], the bread
- Ho Zon [2198], the living

Living Bread speaks of His incarnation, walking among us. "Bread" in both Hebrew and Greek could be used to refer to all food and other necessities, not just the loaf of bread that was their staple food. This notion was deeply ingrained in Jesus and his followers, since they were Jewish. In Jesus' day, as now, when a Jewish person gives thanks to God for "bringing forth bread from the earth," he knows that the blessing covers all food served at that meal. If no bread is served at a meal, the observant Jewish person must then thank God for each item served.

Lamp, Light

*Your word is a **LAMP** unto my feet and a **LIGHT** unto my path.* (Psalm 119:105)
- Ner [5216], lamp
- Or [216], to be or become light

*This one came for a witness, that he might witness about **THE LIGHT** in order that all might believe through Him.* (John 1:7)
- Tou Photos [5457], the light

John is writing about the role of John the Baptist in heralding the appearance of Jesus, the true Light.

Daystar

- *And we have the more established prophetic word, in which you do well to take heed, as to a lamp shining in a murky place, until day dawns, and (the) **DAYSTAR** rises in your hearts:* (2 Peter 1:19)
- Phosphoros [5459], Daystar, Morning Star, light bringing

The First and Last, Living One

*And when I saw Him, I fell toward His feet as dead, and He placed His right hand upon me saying "Stop being afraid! I AM **THE FIRST AND THE LAST** (Isa. 44:6; 48:12) 18. and the **ONE WHO IS LIVING**. And I died, but look! I am living forever and I have the keys of death and Hades..* (Revelation 1:17,18)

- Ho Protos [4413], the first
- Ho Eschatos [2078], the last
- Ho Zon [2222], the living one

He is the First, with God from the beginning. And He is the Last, to reign through eternity. He is the Living One, Who died for us, then rose, that we too could have eternal life. The next few verses strengthen this theme.

The Head, Beginning, Firstborn Out From the Dead, First

*..and He is **THE HEAD** of the body, of the congregation: Who was in the beginning, **FIRSTBORN OUT FROM THE DEAD**, so that He would be **FIRST** in all things,* (Colossians 1:18)

- He Kefale [2776], head, as supreme, chief, prominent, of a person as master or lord
- Arche [746], beginning, origin

- Protokos [4416], firstborn
- Ek [1537], out from
- Ton Nekron [3498], the dead
- Proteuon [4409], to be first, hold the first place, be pre-eminent

As Firstborn from the Dead He is described as the first to have overcome death, to have shown us the way to eternal life. He was resurrected to pave the way for our resurrection, that each of us has overcome death.
(See 1 Corinthians 15:35-58)

The Alef and the Tav, The Lord of Hosts, The Almighty
*I AM **THE ALEF AND THE TAV**, says the Lord God, the One Who is and Who was and Who is coming, **THE LORD OF HOSTS, THE ALMIGHTY**.* (Revelation 1:8)

Alef, first letter of the Hebrew alphabet. The Greek text has Alpha, first letter of the Greek alphabet

Tav, last letter of the Hebrew alphabet. The Greek text has Omega, last letter of the Greek alphabet
- Ho Pantokrator [3841], used in the Septuagint to translate the Hebrew for Lord of Hosts. The Greek word means: he who holds sway over all things, the ruler of all, almighty

In Hebrew the alef and tav form a word used before the direct object of the verb to signify the completion of the action. Jesus is not only the First and Last, but He has completed all things necessary for our living victorious lives. The word Pantokrator was used in the Septuagint for Lord of Hosts.

Beginning and the End
*Then He said to me, "It has been done! I AM the Alef and the Tav, the **BEGINNG AND THE END**. I shall give freely from the fountain of the water of life to the one who thirsts."*
(Revelation 21:6)

The First and the Last
Thus says the LORD* the King of Israel and its Redeemer, the LORD* of Hosts. I AM the FIRST! I AM the LAST! Besides Me there is no God! (Is 44:6, 48:12) I will give freely from the fountain of the water of life to the one who thirsts. (Is 55:1)
  - He Arche [746], the beginning, origin
  - To Telos [5056], the end, termination

First and the Last
Who has appointed and done, calling forth the generations from the beginning? I the LORD* (the) FIRST AND THE LAST. I AM He. (Isaiah 41:4)
  - Rishon [7218], first (derived from Rosh, head
  - Aharonim [314], last

Rishon is an interesting idiom, derived from Rosh, meaning "head" the same Strong's number as Rishon. Rosh HaShanna, translates as "New Year," but literally is "Head the Year."

The Amen, Faithful and True Witness, The Head
And to the angel of the congregation in Laodicea write, These things says THE AMEN, THE FAITHFUL AND TRUE WITNESS, THE HEAD of the creation of God: (Revelation 3:14)
  - Amen [543], not a Hebrew word, but an acrostic, El Melekh N'eman for God is a Faithful King.
  - Ho Martus [3144], witness
  - Ho Pistos [4103], the trusty, faithful, of God abiding by His promises
  - Alethinos [228], that which has not only the name and semblance, but the real nature corresponding to the idea signified by the name, real and true, genuine. (New Thayer Greek-English Lexicon) It is also used in reference to gold.
  - He Arche [746], beginning, here as head

Amen is universally considered to mean "True" or "So be it." However, there is no Hebrew root with the letters Alef-Mem-

Nun. True and truth have the root Alef-MeTav. "So be it" is a translation of the Greek Genoito.

The above use of arche speaks of Jesus as the Word Who was with God the Father in the very beginning. The essence of the word arche deals with origins. Thus we have the opposite, earliest end of the time element.

Heir

*On the last of these days, He spoke to us through a Son, Whom He appointed **HEIR** of all, through Whom He also made the universe.* (Hebrews 1:2)
- Kleronomon [2818], heir

"Heir" refers to the one who receives his allotted possession by right of sonship: so of Messiah, as "Heir of All," all things being subject to Him; of Christians, as exalted sons of Abraham and thus sons of God, due to receive the blessings of God's kingdom promised to Abraham.

We see in these next verses further evidence of His authority as king.

Ruler of the Kings of the Earth

*..and from Jesus Messiah, the Faithful Witness, Firstborn from the dead (Ps 89:28) and the **RULER OF THE KINGS OF THE EARTH**. To the One Who loves us and has loosed us from our sins (Ps 130:8, Is 40:2) by His blood,* (Revelation 1:5)
- Ho Archon [758], the ruler, chief, commander, leader
- Ton Basileuon [935], leader of the people, prince, commander, lord of the land, king
- Ges [1093], earth, arable land

Lord of Lords, King of Kings

*These will make war with the Lamb and the Lamb will overcome them because He is **LORD OF LORDS AND KING OF KINGS**, and those with Him are called and chosen and faithful.* (Revelation 17:14)

- Kurios [2962], lord
- Kurion [2962], of lords
- Basileus [935], king
- Basileon [935], of kings

King of Kings and Lord of Lords
..and He has upon His garment, even over His thigh a name that has been written: 'KING OF KINGS AND LORD OF LORDS.' (Revelation 19:16)
- Basileus [935], king
- Basileon [935], of kings
- Kurios [2962], lord
- Kurion [2962], of lords

Head of All Principality and Authority
..and you must constantly be filled through Him, Who is the HEAD OF EVERY PRINCIPALITY AND AUTHORITY. (Colossians 2:10)
- Kephale [2776], head
- Arches [746], rule
- Exousias [1849], authority

Arches, here translated rule, is also translated head in Revelation 3:14. Its primary meaning is "beginning," but in this instance is used in reference to His being first in a line of authority.

One Ruling
And you Bethlehem Ephrata, being least among the thousands of Judah, out of you He shall come forth to Me to become ONE RULING in Israel and His forthcomings (have been) from of old, from the days of eternity. (Micah 5:2)
- Moshel [4910], one ruling

Judge
..and He commanded us to preach to the people and to testify earnestly that He is the One Who has been appointed by God as JUDGE of the living and the dead. (Acts 10:42)
- Krites [2923], judge

This refers to Jesus' returning to sit in judgment. (See also 2 Timothy 4:8 and James 5:9.) "Judge" speaks of authority, the same as that of a ruler or king. The Bible does not have a man-made system of checks and balances, but all rule and authority come from above.

That is why Moses, Joshua, Caleb, and each of the God appointed judges both ruled and judged simultaneously. The following six verses speak of the reigning Messiah, Who is about to return to rule and reign with us for a thousand years. The One Who was born in Bethlehem two thousand years ago, was foretold by Micah (Micah 5:2) during the reign of Hezekiah more than seven hundred years before the birth of Messiah. He Who was with us and is still with us.

Imanu-el - God is With Us
*Therefore the Lord Himself will give you a sign. Behold, the young woman will bear a son and she will call His name **IMANUEL**.* (Isaiah 7:14)
   - Imanu, [no Strong's #] with us
   - El, [6005], God

In Hebrew Imanuel is one word and speaks of His abiding presence. One of the most comforting aspects of God is that He is with us. He knows where we are and what we are going through. He Who has more compassion than any earthly parent, Who hurts when we hurt and rejoices when we rejoice. As the compassionate Jesus assured us, "*I AM With You.. *"

The word translated Young Woman means an unmarried young woman, who would have been stoned in ancient Israel. The miracle of her delivery of a baby named God With Us is the sign referred to in this verse. In modern Hebrew this word, Almah, means virgin, but it did not have that meaning in Isaiah's day, although an Almah had to be a virgin.

With You
Therefore when you go, you must now make disciples of all the heathens, 20. teaching them to keep all the things that I have

*been commanding you: and behold I AM **WITH YOU** all the days until the end of the age.* (Matthew 28:19,20)
- Ego [1473], I
- Eimi [1510], I am
- Meth [3326], with (the Greek translation of Ima)
- Humon [5216], you

The all-powerful I AM is with you whatever your circumstances.

I AM

*And Jesus spoke to them at once saying, 'You must be courageous! **I AM**! Stop being afraid!'* (Matthew 14:27)
- Ego [1473], I
- Eimi [1510], I am

Ego Eimi is the Greek equivalent of the Hebrew Ani or Anokhi. Hebrew is the language Jesus would have spoken. Jesus is reminding those in the boat that He is God Incarnate! If those who accompanied Him needed to be reminded, how many times do we, who do not see Him, need to be reminded that He is always with us and will never leave us or forsake us?

The term Ego Eimi is used about forty times in the Gospels.

Husband

*And it happened when Joshua was by Jericho, that he lifted up his eyes and looked and, behold, there was a **HUSBAND** standing opposite him with His sword drawn in His hand. And Joshua went to Him and said to Him, Are you for us, or for our adversaries?* (Joshua 5:13)
- Ish [376], husband, man

The word "husband" was used in this translation to emphasize the role of the Messiah as the Bridegroom. The Hebrew word used is "Ish," one of the words used for husband. Here this has to be Jesus, the only angelic being with the potential of being a husband, a bridegroom. This is the One Who wrestled with

Jacob (Genesis 32:25). See also Matthew 9:15, Mark 2:19, Luke 5:34. The very next verse, Joshua 5:14, tells of His authority.

The Captain of (the) Army

*And He said, No, but I have come as **Captain of the Army of The LORD***. And Joshua fell on his face to the earth, and worshipped and said to Him, What does my Lord say to His servant?* (Joshua 5:14)
- Sar [8269], prince
- Tseva [6635], army, host

The root of Tseva is ts-v-a [6633], meaning to wage war, to serve. Thus, the commonly used phrase "Lord of Hosts" always refers to the army of the Lord, and also to His warfare that makes us victorious. In these last days we need to be increasingly aware of this warfare, not only to win the victory in which we should live, but more importantly, to prepare the bride. We need to concentrate on the glorious congregation that He is coming to claim, *in order that He would present for Himself the glorious congregation, not having spot or wrinkle or any of such things, but so that His bride would be holy and without blemish.* (Ephesians 5:27) Only when the members of the Body of Messiah stand together without spot or wrinkle: only then can we expect the Bridegroom to come.

The Bridegroom

*And Y'shua said to them, 'Are the sons of the bridechamber able to mourn as long as **THE BRIDEGROOM** is with them? But days will come when **THE BRIDEGROOM** will be taken away from them and then they will fast.'* (Matthew 9:15)
- Ho Numphios [3566], the bridegroom

Lord of Glory

*..which none of the leaders of this age knew: for if they had known, they would not have crucified **THE LORD OF GLORY***. (1 Corinthians 2:8)
- Ton Kurion [2462], master, lord
- Tes Doxes [1391], opinion, judgment, splendor, brightness, Glory

In the Septuagint and others Doxes is a translation of the Hebrew word "Kavod" [3519], meaning abundance, honor, glory. A single verse of scripture introduces the next four names.

Wonder, Counselor, Mighty God, Everlasting Father, Prince of Peace

For unto us a child is born, unto us a Son is given, and the government is upon His shoulder, and His name will be called ***WONDER, COUNSELOR, MIGHTY GOD, EVERLASTING FATHER, PRINCE OF PEACE.*** (Isaiah 9:5)
- Pele [6382], miracle, wonder: Pele is a noun, but is often translated as an adjective "wonderful."
- Yo-ets [3289], advice, counsel
- Gibor [1368], strong, mighty
- El [410], God, El speaks of power
- Olam [5769]. eternal, everlasting
- Avi [1], my father
- Ad [5703], pass on, advance
- Sar [8269], prince
- Shalom [7965], peace, completeness, soundness, welfare

The root of Shalom is sh-l-m [7999], meaning to be complete, sound, secure, make over, to be in a covenant of peace. That says much more than we can put into one word.

This is one of the richest verses we have describing the coming Messiah. The next verse, also from Isaiah, predicts the Messiah's lineage, well over 700 years before His birth!

Shoot, Branch

*And there will come forth a **SHOOT** out of the trunk of Jesse, and a **BRANCH** will grow out of his roots:* (Isaiah 11:1)
- Hoter [2415], shoot, branch, twig, rod
- Netser [5342], branch, sprout

These two words speak of His flesh, His manhood. Joseph's lineage went back through David to Jesse (David's father), who lived over a thousand years before the birth of Jesus. Netser is the source of the name

Nazareth, which is Natseret in Hebrew. That is why Matthew 2:23 says *and when he came he dwelt in a city called Nazareth: thus was the word through the prophet fulfilled that He will be called of Nazareth.*

Your Right Hand

*Return, we beseech You, O God of Hosts. Look down from heaven and see and visit this vine, 16. and the plant which **YOUR RIGHT HAND** has set and the branch You made strong for Yourself.* (Psalm 80:15,16)
- Yemine-kha [3225], your right hand

David here prophesied Jesus' position when the Father seated *Him* on His right hand in the heavenlies (Ephesians 1:20)

The Right Hand speaks of power and strength, from Exodus 15:6.

Man (Husband) of Your Right Hand, Son of Man

*Let Your hand be on the **MAN OF YOUR RIGHT HAND**, upon the **SON OF MAN** Whom You made strong for Yourself.* (Psalm 80:18)
- Ish, [376], man, husband
- Yemine-kha [3225], your right hand
- Ben [1121], son
- Adam [120], man, mankind

The right hand is a Hebrew expression that speaks of power and strength, taken from Exodus 15:6 and Deuteronomy 33:2. The right hand also symbolizes God's salvation, from Psalm 20:6, while the left hand symbolizes calamity and judgment.

Son of Man uses the most common Hebrew word for man, adam, which can also mean "mankind." Son of Man was frequently used in Jesus' day to speak of Messiah. The next verse uses the Aramaic words for Son of Man.

Son of Man

I saw visions in the night and, behold, one like a SON OF MAN (Rev. 1:13; 4:14) came with the clouds of heaven (Matt. 24:30, Mark 14:62, Luke 21:27, Acts 1:9-11) and came to the Ancient of Days and they brought Him near before Him. (Daniel 7:13)
- Kevar [1247], like a son
- Enash [606], man, mankind

The "K" prefix of kevar translates as the preposition "like." Without the prefix it would be "bar," as in "Simon Bar Jonah."

Root of Jesse

And in that Day there will be a ROOT OF JESSE Who will stand for a sign, miracle, for the peoples. To Him will the nations seek, and His resting place will be glorious. (Isaiah 11:10)
- Shoresh [8328], root
- Yishai [3448], Jesse

This verse establishes that the Messiah is not only a descendent but also an ancestor of Jesse.

The next verse emphasizes a trait that Jesus requires of every Christian. *Whoever wishes to be great among you must be your servant.* (Matthew 20:26)

My Servant, My Elect

Behold MY SERVANT, whom I uphold; MY ELECT, in whom My very being delights. I have put My Spirit upon Him. He will bring forth judgment to the nations. (Isaiah 42:1)
- Avdi [5650], my slave, my servant
- Behiri [972], my chosen

The obedience of Jesus was truly astonishing. He was at the Father's service continuously, and walked in the anointing of the Holy Spirit constantly, as only God Incarnate could.

My Shepherd, My Associate

Awake, O sword, against MY SHEPHERD and against MY ASSOCIATE, says the LORD* of Hosts. Strike the shepherd and the sheep will be scattered (Matt. 26:31, Mark 14:27), and I shall turn My hand against the little ones. (Zechariah 13:7)
- Ro-i [7462], my shepherd, figurative of Jesus as ruler
- Gever [1397], man (as strong)
- Amiti [5997], my associate, my relation

Jesus cited this verse:
*Then Jesus said to them, "You all will be caused to sin this night because of Me, for it has been written, 'I will strike the **Shepherd**, and the sheep of the flock will be scattered.' (Zechariah 13:7) 32. But after My resurrection I will meet you in Galilee.* (Matthew 26:31,32)

God refers to the Messiah as My Shepherd and My Associate, Emphasizing their relationship. Gever stresses strength as its root, g-v-r [1396] means to be strong, mighty.

Notice the different words that have been translated "Man." Adam and Enosh mean "man, mankind." Ish emphasizes husband, with that intimate partnership, and Gever shows His strength, that all things are possible through Him. The Greek word for man, mankind is anthropos, comparable to the Hebrew word, adam, and for husband, man, aner is equivalent to ish.

Jeremiah is the first to use the next name, in a prayer; Paul again identifies it 700 years later.

Hope of Israel, Savior

O, HOPE OF ISRAEL, its SAVIOR in time of trouble, why should You be like a stranger in the land and as a wayfaring man who turns aside to tarry a night? (Jeremiah 14:8)

- Mikveh [4723], hope
- Yisrael [3478], Israel, contended with God
- Moshi-o [3467], its helper, savior, deliverer

The root of Mikveh is k-v-h [6960], meaning to wait for, to look for. Many to whom Paul spoke had been waiting for Messiah, looking for Him for years. He was their Hope, as He is the Hope of many Jewish people looking for Him today. Christians too await the imminent return of Messiah.

The Hope of Israel
*For the sake of this cause then I called for you to see and to speak (to you); because of **THE HOPE OF ISRAEL**,* (Acts 28:20)
- Tes Elpidos [1680], the hope, expectation of good
- Tou Israel [2474], of the Israel

Righteous Sprout
Behold, days are coming, says the LORD, that I shall raise a **RIGHTEOUS SPROUT**, Y'shua, for David and He will reign as king and succeed and will execute justice and acts of loving kindness in the earth.* (Jeremiah 23:5)
- Tsemah [6780], sprout, growth
- Tsadik [6666], righteous

Our Righteousness
In His days Judah will be saved and Israel will dwell safely, and this is His name by which He will be called, The LORD **OUR RIGHTEOUSNESS**.* (Jeremiah 23:6)
- Tsidkenu [6666], our righteousness

The root of Tsadik and Tsidkenu is ts-d-k [6663], which means to be just, to be righteous. This virtue requires action, to treat all in a just way. This Hebrew name for God the Son has its equivalent in the Greek of the New Testament, as used in the next example.

The Just One
*Which of the prophets did your fathers not persecute? And they killed those who before did announce concerning **THE RIGHTEOUS ONE**, of Whom you now have become betrayers and murderers.* (Acts 7:52)
- Tou Dikaiou [1342], righteous, observing divine and human laws, one who is "such as he ought to be," observant of the custom, usage.

Righteousness requires action: to observe the laws, to be what God would have us to be.

Upright One
*The way of the righteous is 'uprightness.' You, **UPRIGHT ONE**, do weigh the path of the righteous.* (Isaiah 26:7)
- Yashar [3474], to be smooth, straight, right

Sun of Acts of Loving Kindness
*But to you who revere My name, the **SUN OF ACTS OF LOVING KINDNESS** will rise with healing in His wings and you will go out and prosper like attending calves in the stall.* (Malachi 3:20)
- Shemesh [8121], sun
- Tsedakah [6666], acts of loving kindness.

Righteouness is the translation of Tsedek, which is God's minimum standard. Tsedakah means to go beyond His minimum and should be translated Acts of Loving Kindness.

Read also 2 Samuel 15:4 and Psalm 82:3 where the call is clearly to do justice. God's cry throughout His Word is to do His commands. (See Deuteronomy 28:1,2,9,13, Matthew 7:21, Romans 2:6, James 1:22.) You must love your neighbor as yourself (Leviticus 19:18, Matthew 22:39), a requirement that we do justice.

Stone, Tried Stone, Precious Cornerstone, Sure Foundation
Therefore thus says Adonai, the LORD, Behold, I lay for a foundation in Zion a **STONE**, a **TRIED STONE**, a **PRECIOUS CORNERSTONE**, a **SURE FOUNDATION**. He who believes will not make haste.* (Isaiah 28:16)
- Aven [68], stone
- Ehven [68], stone
- Bohan [976], testing, approved for use as a foundation stone
- Yikrat [3368], precious
- Pinah [6438], corner
- Musad [4143], foundation

Pinah is used as a figure of a ruler or chief (Judges 20:2, 1 Samuel 14:38, Isaiah 19:13, Zechariah 10:4.) The root is p-n-h [6437], to turn. This is a picture of Jesus as the foundation of the Body of Messiah.

But Jesus is not just any of the foundation stones, He is the . . .

Cornerstone, Head Cornerstone
*Because also it is contained in Scripture 'Behold I place in Zion a stone, a valuable, chosen **CORNERSTONE**, and the one who believes in Him will **not** be put to sham. Therefore for you who believe, He is precious, but with the disbelieving, He is a Stone that the builders rejected, This One became **HEAD CORNERSTONE**.'* (1 Peter 2:6,7)
- Akrogoniaion [204], placed at the extreme corner, speaking of Messiah
- Kephalen [2776], head, here metaphorically as supreme, chief, prominent
- Gonias [1137], an external angle, the head of the corner

Both these words translated "cornerstone" represent the cornerstone: that which holds together two walls: a picture of Messiah joining together those who are Jewish and those who were formerly heathens into one body dedicated to God.

The Stone

*This is **THE STONE** counted worthless by you the builders, Who has become Head of the corner, and there is salvation in no other One, for neither is there another name under heaven having been given among men by which we must be saved.* (Acts 4:11,12)
- Ho Lithos [3037], stone

Stone of Stumbling, Rock of Offence

*And He will be a Sanctuary (John 2:19-21), but for a **STONE OF STUMBLING** and for a **ROCK OF OFFENCE** to both the houses of Israel, for a trap and a snare to the inhabitants of Jerusalem.* (Isaiah 8:14)
- Ehven [68], stone
- Negef [5062], striking, against which the foot strikes and so stumbles
- Tsur [6697], rock, cliff
- Mikshol [4383], stumbling

Ehven means "small stone," but it often refers to a cut stone (the sort used in construction). It can also refer to a cut jewel, a gemstone. Tsur refers to a huge rocky cliff. (See Chapter 10, Refuge, for additional uses of this word.)

Paul referred to this same passage (Isaiah 8:14) in his letter to the Romans.

Stone of Stumbling, Rock of Offense

*For they stumbled at the **STONE OF STUMBLING**, even as it was, behold I place in Zion a **STONE OF STUMBLING** and a **ROCK OF OFFENSE**, and everyone believing on Him will not be put to shame.*
(Romans 9:33)
- Lithon [3037], stone
- Proskommatos [4348], stumbling block

- Petran [4073], rock, ledge, cliff, large stone
- Scandalou [4625], the movable stick or trigger of a snare or trap

The expressions Stone of Stumbling and Rock of Offense are used as a figure of Jesus Whose person and career were so contrary to the expectations of the Jewish people concerning the Messiah, that they rejected Him. (J H Thayer)

When Jesus was born, Israel had been under Greek or Roman control for over 300 years, and had enjoyed just a few brief periods of religious freedom. There were only four years of Jewish autonomy following the successful Maccabean revolt of 164 BC, and the last two years of that were spent under siege. Then in 160 BC Judas Maccabeus was defeated and killed. Under Greek rule there was so much oppression that the Jewish people believed that the coming Messiah had to be the conquering Messiah, the reigning King of Kings. That presumption resulted in their being blinded for a time (Romans 11:8).

For I do not want you to be ignorant, brothers, of this mystery, lest you become conceited, because insensibility in part has come upon Israel until the fullness of the heathens would come in (Lk 21:24) *26. and in this way all Israel will be saved, just as it has been written, 'The One Who rescues will come out of Zion, He will banish ungodliness from Jacob. 27. and this is the covenant for them with Me, when I would take away their sins.'* (Isaiah 59:20,21, from Romans 11:25-27)

Your King, Humble
*Rejoice very exuberantly, O daughter of Zion! Shout, O daughter of Jerusalem! Behold, **YOUR KING** will come to you. He is just and having victory, **HUMBLE** and riding on a donkey, even on a colt, the foal of a donkey.* (Zechariah 9:9)
- Malkekh [4428], your king
- Ani [6041], to be bowed down, afflicted

This is the first Scripture to call Jesus King and also the first to call Him Humble! His kingship is expressed by Pilate, as recorded in all four gospels, (Matthew 27:37, Mark 15:26,32, Luke 23:38, John 19:19-22).

The King of the Jewish People

*And Pilate also wrote an inscription and placed it on the cross: and it was written, 'Y'shua of Nazareth, **THE KING OF THE JEWISH PEOPLE**.' 20. Therefore many of the Jewish people read this inscription, because the place where Jesus was crucified was near the city: and it was written in Hebrew, Roman, and Greek. 21. Then the high priests of the Jewish people were saying to Pilate, 'You must not write, "The King of the Jewish People," but that "That One said, 'I am King of the Jewish People.'"' 22. Pilate answered, 'What I have written, I have written.'* (John 19:19-22)
- Ho Basileus [935], the king
- Ton Ioudaion [2453], of the Jews

He must truly be the King for each one of us, if we are to live in love and to be all that He wants us to be.

The next verse continues this theme, Jesus' kingship, but now we also return to the theme introduced by Jacob (in Genesis 49:8). He used the word Shiloh in speaking of the One men try to reach, and this next verse uses a Greek word speaking of that same One.

The One Coming

*For yet a very little while and **THE ONE COMING** will come, and not delay;* (Hebrews 10:37)
- Ho Erchomenos [2064], the one coming

The author of Hebrews is citing Habakkuk 2:3, referring to Jesus. The more commonly used word today is "Messiah." In Old Testament days He was normally referred to by other names. (This helps explain why this chapter is so large. More than fifty of His names come from the Hebrew Scriptures.) The first of these references is from the New Testament, but we do find the word Messiah in the Greek as well.

The Messiah, The King of Israel

And likewise also the chief priests with the scribes said, mocking, to one another; 'He saved others but He is not able to save Himself: THE MESSIAH; THE KING OF ISRAEL, must now come down from the cross, so that we would see and we would believe..' (Mark 15:31,32)
- Ho Christos [5547], the Messiah
- Ho Basileus [935], the king
- Israel [2474], Israel

Lord of All

The message which He sent to the children of Israel, when He proclaimed Good News of peace through Y'shua Messiah, this One is LORD OF ALL. (Acts 10:36)
- Panton [3956], of all
- Kurios [2062], lord

He is definitely the King of Israel and the Lord of All. He came to bring God's redemptive power and love to all mankind, as He said in John 10:16. *But I also have sheep which are not from this sheepfold: and it is necessary for Me to lead those and they will hear My voice, and they will become one flock, one Shepherd.*

When He comes Christians and the Jewish people will see the same Messiah, Who will meld us all into one body.

Messiah

And Jacob begat Joseph the husband of Miriam, out of whom was born Y'shua, the One called MESSIAH. (Matthew 1:16)
- Christos [5547], Messiah, Anointed One

The Mashiakh

*..first he found his own brother Simon, then said to him, 'We have found **THE MASHIAH**,' which is translated Messiah:* (John 1:41)

      - Ton Messian [3323], the Messiah (see also John 4:25)

Mashiah is the English spelling of the Hebrew word found in Daniel 9:25.

Mashiah Prince

*Know therefore and understand, that from the going forth of the commandment to restore and to build Jerusalem until the **MASHIAH PRINCE** will be seven weeks: and during sixty-two weeks it will be built again, with street and trench, even in troubled times.* (Daniel 9:25)

      - Mashiah [4899], anointed, messiah
      - Nagid [5057], prince

"Weeks" here refers to weeks of years (one week equals seven years.) Daniel was prophesying the time-span from the order by Cyrus to rebuild Jerusalem to the birth of Mashiakh Prince. Our English, Messiah, is a transliteration of the Greek spelling of Mashiakh.

My Messiah

*There I shall make the horn of David to bud: I have ordained a lamp for **MY MESSIAH**.* (Psalm 132:17)

      - M'shihi [4899], My Messiah

This last verse states clearly the connection between Messiah and David. "Horn" speaks of His strength. "Sprout" indicates that the Messiah will come through David's lineage.

Nahum depicts the Son in the role as the One bringing Good News.

Who Brings Good News
*Behold, upon the mountains are the feet of him **WHO BRINGS
GOOD NEWS** Who is declaring Shalom! O Judah, keep your
solemn feasts! Perform your vows! For the wicked one will no
longer pass through you. He is utterly cut off.* (Nahum 2:1)
- Mevaser [1319], one bringing good news

This same title is also found in Isaiah 52:7. The root word, b-s-r
[1319] means to bear glad tidings, clearly a call for the One, the
Name above all names, referred to by the High Priest in Acts
5:28. See Name on page 21.

The next verse takes its cue from Psalm 132:17, referring to
Messiah's strength and to His lineal relationship to David. See
Good News in the Glossary of the One New Man Bible.

The Lion of the Tribe of Judah, The Root of David
*And one of the elders said to me, 'Stop weeping! Look! He was
victorious, **THE LION OF THE TRIBE OF JUDAH**, (Gn
49:9,10) **THE ROOT OF DAVID**, (Is 11:1) so He can open the
scroll and its seven seals.* (Revelation 5:5)
- Ho Le-on [3023], the lion
- Ho on [5607], who is
- Ek [1537], out from
- Tes Fules [5443], the tribe
- Iouda [2455], of Judah
- He Riza [4491], the root
- Dauid [1138], David

This verse differs from Psalm 132 in that Messiah is here
described as an ancestor (root) of David instead of a descendant.
"Lion" is an appropriate title for One of ultimate strength and
authority, at the right hand of the Father.

Notice that the Greek word for David is written Dauid. The
"u" was used to represent the Hebrew letter vav because there
is no "v" in Koine Greek. Another Hebrew letter pronounced

like a v is the vet, which is written in Greek as a "b." That gives us Iacob instead of Yaakov, the Hebrew spelling, with the English spelling taking its cue from the Greek and Latin, not the Hebrew.

Lamb
*And I saw, and behold, in (the) midst of the throne, and amidst the elders, a **LAMB** standing as having been slain, having seven horns and seven eyes, which are the seven Spirits of God, that were sent into all the earth.* (Revelation 5:6)
- Arnion [721], lamb

The Lamb
*On the next day John sees Jesus coming toward him, and says, 'Behold, **THE LAMB** of God, Who takes away the sin of the world.'* (John 1:29)
- Ho Amnos [286], the lamb

He is both the Lion (Victorious, Powerful, Almighty) and the sacrificial Lamb, Who died that we might have eternal life.

These two Greek words, arnion and amnos, for lamb are synonymous, but amnos is the more commonly used.

The next verses deal with His humanity and His human lineage.

Firstborn
*And she did bear her Son, **THE FIRSTBORN**; and she wrapped Him in the manger, because there was not room for them in the inn.* (Luke 2:7)
- Ton Proton [4416], the firstborn
- He is the Firstborn Son of the Father, God Incarnate.

Son of Abraham
*A scroll of the genealogy of Y'shua Messiah, Son of David, **SON OF ABRAHAM**.* (Matthew 1:1)
- Huiou [5207], son of
- Abraham [11], Abraham

Son of David

*And there was a Canaanite woman from those regions, when she came out and she cried out saying; 'You must have mercy on me right now, Lord, **SON OF DAVID**! My daughter has an evil spirit.'* (Matthew 15:22)
- Huios [5207], son
- Dauid [1138], David

The Root and the Offspring of David, The Bright Morning Star

*I, Y'shua, did send My messenger to testify these things for the congregations. I AM **THE ROOT AND THE OFFSPRING OF DAVID, THE BRIGHT MORNING STAR**.* (Revelation 22:16)
- He Riza [4491], the root
- Kai To Genos [1085], and the offspring
- Dauid [1138], David
- Ho Aster [792], the star
- Ho Lampros [2986], the bright
- Ho Pro-inos [3720], the morning

He is flesh, the Son of David, Son of Abraham, and at the same time God, with the Father from the very beginning, so He is, simultaneously, both the Root and the Offspring of David. He is and always has been the

Bright Morning Star.

My Son

*And He was there until the death of Herod: so that the word of the Lord by the prophet would be fulfilled, saying ` I called **MY SON** out of Egypt.* (Matthew 2:15)
- Ton Huion [5207], the son
- Mou [3450], of me

My Son
> *When Israel was a young man I loved him, and called MY SON out of Egypt.* (Hosea 11:1)
>> - Livni [1121], to my son

The "L" is a prefix translated "to." Without the prefix it would be "Beni" as "My Son".

The Son of the Living God
> *And Simon Peter said, 'You are the Messiah, THE SON OF THE LIVING GOD.' 17. and Y'shua said to him, 'Blessed are you Simon Bar-Jonah, because not flesh and blood, but My Father in the heavens revealed this to you,'* (Matthew 16:16)
>> - Ho Huios [5207], the son
>> - Tou The-ou [2316], the God
>> - Tou Zontos [2226], the living

Son of the Most High
> *This One will be great, and will be called SON OF THE MOST HIGH and the Lord God will give Him the throne of David His father.* (Luke 1:32)
>> - Huios [5207], son
>> - Hupsistou [5310], of most high

This verse speaks of His Messianic reign, and is amplified in the next verse, Luke 1:33 *and He will reign over the house of Jacob forever, and His kingdom will not end.*

The Lord of the Harvest
> *Pray for THE LORD OF THE HARVEST, that He may send workmen into His harvest.* (Matthew 9:38)
>> - Tou Kurion [2962], lord
>> - Tou Therismou [2362], of the harvest

Son of Man, Lord of the Sabbath
> *For THE SON OF MAN is LORD OF THE SABBATH.* (Matthew 12:8)

- Ho Huios [5207], the son
- Tou Anthropou [444], of the man
- Kurios [2962], lord
- Tou Sabbatou [4521], of the Sabbath

Not only is He the Lord of the Harvest and of the Sabbath, the following scriptures establish Him as the Master.

The Master
*But false prophets were also among the people, as even false teachers will be among you, who will bring destruction by their opinions, even denying **THE MASTER**, the One Who purchased them. Although they quickly bring utter destruction on themselves,* (2 Peter 2:1)
- Ton Despoten [1203], the master, lord

Master
*And went to Him they woke Him, saying '**MASTER, MASTER!** We are being destroyed!' Then after He got up He rebuked the wind and the wave of the water: and it stopped and it was calm.* (Luke 8:24)
- Epistata [1988], master, any type of superintendent or overseer

Clearly, He must be Master of our lives. Each one of us must submit totally to Him, yielding all our pride, all our accomplishments, and all our possessions to Him.

Dayspring
*Through (the) heart of mercy of our God, by means of which (the) **DAYSPRING** from on high will visit us.* (Luke 1:78)
- Anatole [395], dayspring, a rising

The word "heart" is the translation of the Greek word splanchna [4698], sometimes translated "bowels" or "inward parts." In Hebrew, however, it corresponds to the way we use "heart" in modern English, meaning, "the seat of tender affections.. kindness, benevolence, compassion." (J H Thayer)

Comforter of Israel

And behold a man by the name of Simeon was in Jerusalem and this righteous and devout man, was waiting for the **COMFORTER OF ISRAEL** *and the Holy Spirit was upon him.* (Luke 2:25)

- Paraklesin [3874], consolation, comfort, refreshing, of solace: Rabbis call the Messiah the Consoler, the Comforter
- Tou Israel [2474], of the Israel

Paraklesin is a feminine noun also used in reference to the Holy Spirit in Acts 9:31. A related word Parakletos [3875], meaning intercessor, mediator, comforter, advocate, is used five times in the New Testament – four times referring to the Holy Spirit (see Chapter 2, page 13. The Scriptures referring to the Holy Spirit are: John 14:15, 16, & 26, and John 16:7, and once referring to Jesus, 1 John 2:1).

The Teacher

While He was yet speaking someone came to Him from the synagogue ruler saying to him, 'Your daughter has died, do not trouble **THE TEACHER**.*'"* (Luke 8:49)

- Ton Didaskalon [1320], the teacher

There were a number of rabbis who walked the length and breadth of Israel teaching disciples. In fact the Hebrew word translated "disciples," mudim, means "those who are taught." Jesus taught with notable authority (Matthew 7:29, Mark 1:22). Remember that the role of the shepherd, when dealing with people, requires teaching. What did He teach? He taught the Torah, the Scriptures, relating the Word of the Lord to everyday life. Torah means "Teaching."

The next Scripture portrays Him in another of His roles, the Lamb of God.

Passover
> *You must immediately cleanse the old leaven, so that you would be a new lump, just as you are unleavened: for also our* **PASSOVER** *Messiah was sacrificed.* (1 Corinthians 5:7)
>   - Pascha [3958], Passover

Pascha is the Greek spelling of the Hebrew word Pesa<u>h</u>, meaning "pass over" in reference to the angel of death. However, it was also commonly used in speaking of the animal used for the sacrifice, as here it refers to the Lamb of God.

The next verse speaks of Jesus as our sustenance.

The Bread of Life
> *And Jesus said to them, 'I Myself am* **THE BREAD OF LIFE***: the one coming to Me will not at all hunger, and the one believing in Me will in no way thirst, ever!'* (John 6:35)
>   - Ho Artos [740], the bread
>   - Tes Zo-es [2222], the life

Both these words have much greater depth of meaning than the commonly understood "bread" and "life." Artos, like the Hebrew lekhem, also refers to food of any kind, including spiritual food, the divine word. Zoes, which usually refers to animate life, also speaks of the fullness of spiritual blessings.

The Door
> *Then Jesus said again, "I most definitely say to you that I AM* **THE DOOR** *of the sheep."* (John 10:7)
>   - He Thura [2374], the door

He is The Door, the only way. The next verse tells why.

The Way, The Truth, The Life
> *Jesus said to him, "I AM* **THE WAY** *and* **THE TRUTH** *and* **THE LIFE***: no one comes to the Father except through Me."* (John 14:6)

- He Hodos [3598], the way, frequently used as a figure of speech e.g. a course of conduct (see Chapter 21)
- He Aletheia [225], the truth, in Jesus the sum and personification of truth
- He Zo-e [2222], the life, fullness of spiritual blessings

To go in the Way of Jesus is to copy His obedience, confidence, and continuous communication with the Father.

The Resurrection and the Life

*Jesus said to her, "I AM **THE RESURRECTION AND THE LIFE**: the one who believes in Me, even if he would die, he will live,."* (John 11:25)

- He Anastasis [386], the resurrection, raising up, rising
- He Zo-e [2222], animate life, fullness of spiritual blessings

The Author of Life

*And you killed **THE AUTHOR OF LIFE** Whom God raised out from the dead, of which we are witnesses.* (Acts 3:15)

- Ton Archegon [747], the author, chief leader, prince. This is translated "prince" in Acts 5:31, KJV, NIV, and others.
- Tes Zo-es [2222], animate life, fullness of spiritual blessings

This speaks of His being the Creator as well as the One Who made eternal life available to us.

Guarantee

*By so much then Jesus has become a **GUARANTEE** of a better covenant..* (Hebrews 7:22)

- Engus [1450], surety, guarantee

This is our assurance that He has given us a better covenant, along with all its promises of salvation, deliverance, healing, and victory now guaranteed.

That Prophet

*And it shall be every soul, whoever may not hear **THAT PROPHET**, will be utterly destroyed from that people.* (Acts 3:23)

- Tou Prophetou [4396], the prophet, from prophemi, to speak forth, speak out
- Ekeinou [1565], that

The Spirit of Prophecy

*Then I fell before his feet to pay homage to him. And he said to me, "Stop! Don't do that: I am a fellow servant with you and your brothers who have the testimony of Y'shua: you must now pay homage to God. For the testimony of Y'shua is **THE SPIRIT OF PROPHECY!**"* (Revelation 19:10)

- To Pneuma [4151], the spirit.
- Tes Propheteias [4394], the prophecy, discourse emanating from divine inspiration declaring the purposes of God.

The Holy Spirit is the agent God uses to put prophetic utterances in the mouths of men and women. (See also 1 Thessalonians 5:19, Acts 21:11.)

Seed

*And the promises were spoken to Abraham and to his seed. It does not say, 'And to the seeds,' as upon many but as upon one, 'And to your **SEED**,' (Genesis 13:15) Who is Messiah.* (Galatians 3:16)

- Sperma [4690], seed

The Seed

*Therefore what is the Torah? It was added on account of the transgressions, until **THE SEED** would come for whom it has been promised, since it has been dictated through angels by the hand of a Mediator.* (Galatians 3:19)

- To Sperma [4690], the seed

This again refers to Jesus and to His human nature as a descendant of Abraham.

Savior

*For our citizenship is in the heavens, out from which then we have been waiting eagerly a **SAVIOR** for ourselves, Lord Y'shua Messiah,* (Philippians 3:20)
- Sotera [4990], savior, deliverer

In Hebrew, another word, Goel, is translated Savior or Redeemer.

Mediator

*For there is one God and one **MEDIATOR** between God and mankind, the man Messiah Jesus,* (1 Timothy 2:5)
- Mesites [3316], mediator, one who intervenes between two, either in order to make or restore peace and friendship, or to form a compact.

By His death, Jesus interposed Himself and restored the harmony between God and man – the harmony which human sin had broken.

Advocate

*My little children, I write these things to you so that you would not sin. But if anyone does sin, we have an **ADVOCATE** with the Father, Jesus Messiah, the righteous:* (1 John 2:1)
- Paraklete [3875], called to one's side, intercessor, mediator, comforter, advocate

He is our Advocate, our Comforter, our Intercessor, and our Mediator. When He acts as our Mediator and our Advocate, He does so in the role of our Minister.

The Apostle

*For this reason, holy brothers, sharers of the heavenly calling, you must now consider **THE APOSTLE** and High Priest of our confession, Jesus.*

(Hebrews 3:1)
- Ton Apostolon [652], delegate, messenger, one sent forth

Minister

*One blessed with the holy things, a **MINISTER** of the saints and of the true tabernacle, which the Lord built, not man."*
(Hebrews 8:2)
- Leitourgos [3011], one busied with the holy things, of a priest

Leitourgos is the word from which we get the word liturgy. Continuing with this theme, we now see Jesus as our High Priest, the right hand of the Father.

Priest

The LORD has sworn and He will not repent, You are a **PRIEST** forever after the order of Melchizedek.* (Psalm 110:4)
- Kohen [3548], priest

Forerunner

*Where Jesus entered, a **FORERUNNER**, for us, according to the order of Melchizedek becoming a High Priest to the ages.*
(Hebrews 6:20)
- Prodromos [4274], forerunner

This refers to the one who comes to a place where the rest are to follow. This is the only use of this word in Scripture, and it surely points to the One Whom we will join, to rule and reign for eternity!

High Priest

*But the main thing for those who are being addressed is that we have such a **HIGH PRIEST** Who has sat down on the right hand of the Throne of The Majesty in the heavens.* (Hebrews 8:1)
- Archierea [749], high priest

The Author and Finisher of the Faith

*..fixing our eyes on **THE AUTHOR AND FINISHER OF THE FAITH**, Y'shua, Who, to obtain the joy set before Him, endured the cross, having despised the shame of it He sat down at the right hand of the throne of God.* (Hebrews 12:2)

- Ton Archegon [747], one taking the lead, author
- Tes Pisteos [4102], conviction, belief, holy fervor born of faith and conjoined with it; that God is the provider and bestower of eternal salvation through Messiah.
- Teleioten [5051], a perfecter

This is the only time teleioten is used in the New Testament. It means One Who has in His own Person (the leader or author) raised faith to its perfection and so set before us the highest example of faith (the perfecter).

The Faithful Witness

*..and from Jesus Messiah, **THE FAITHFUL WITNESS**, Firstborn from the dead (Ps 89:27) and the ruler of the kings of the earth. To the One Who loves us and has loosed us from our sins (Ps 130:8, Is 40:2) by His blood,* (Revelation 1:5)

- Ho Martus [3144], the faithful interpreter of God's counsels, a witness
- Ho Pistos [4103], trusty, faithful; worthy of trust; that can be relied on.

The construction in the Greek emphasizes His faithfulness; that we are to depend on Him.

Propitiation

*And He is (the)means by which our sins are forgiven, the **PROPITIATION** concerning our sins: and not concerning ours only but also on behalf of the whole world.* (1 John 2:2)

- Hilasmos [2434], an appeasing, as a priest offering an expiatory sacrifice.
- The Hebrew word for propitiation is Hatat [2403], meaning sin offering. Propitiation is a one-word description of His sacrifice as the Lamb of God.

Your Pious One
*For You will not commit My life to the grave, neither will You permit **YOUR PIOUS ONE** to see corruption.* (Psalm 16:10)
- Hasidyekha [2623], your pious, Godly (as denoting active practice of kindness)

The root is h-s-d [2616], to be good, kind (in eager zeal). Interestingly, David Flusser, in his *Jewish Sources in Early Christianity* devotes an entire chapter, Jesus and Second Temple Pietism, to Jesus and the Hasidim (the Pious). The doctrines taught by Jesus aligned more closely with those of the Hasidim than any other sect at that time. How accurate King David's prophetic words were! (Please note, this is not the same sect called by that name today.) Their doctrines were very similar to those of the Pharisees, excepting the extreme legalism so prevalent among the Pharisees. The names applicable to Jesus completely cover the spectrum, including His relationship to the Father, His eternal nature, possessing all power, His humility, being a servant, even His sacrifice as our Passover.

CHAPTER 4

Living God

Names Introduced in Chapter 4

Living God	El Hai
Living God	Elaha Haya
I Am Who I Am	Ehyeh Asher Ehyeh
I AM	Anokhi
I AM	Ani
My King and My God	Malkhi VElohai
The Man	HaAdam
Your Father	Avi-kha
My Father	Avi
Our Father	Avinu
Our Redeemer, Eternal	Go-elaynu Me-olam
Father	Pater
One Father	Av Ehod
Your Husband	Vo-alaikh
My Husband	Ishi & Ba-ali
Husband	Ish
I Will Make You a People of Covenant	Etenkha Livrite Am

The God we serve is very real, the one true Living God. Scripture further emphasizes this by showing that we are created in His image (Genesis 1:26). As the Living God, He also reminds us that He desires a personal relationship with each one of us. This personal relationship starts with Him: the Living God, Who dwells with us and walks with us continuously. He is eager to spend time with you, but the choice is yours,

He will not force Himself on you.

Living God

*And Joshua said, This is how you will know that the **LIVING GOD** is among you, and He will without fail drive out from before you the Canaanite, the Hittite, the Hivite, the Perizzite, the Girgashite, the Amorite, and the Jebusite.* (Joshua 3:10)

- Hai [2416], alive, living. Used over 50 times referring to God
- El [410], God, El speaks of power

There are many false gods, but nearly all are dead, such as wealth, power, and fame. Some people worship trees or animals, which are alive, but do not have the ability to think or speak. There is only one Supreme Being Who created everything and Who dwells with us and within us, Who Goes Before us and serves as our Rear Guard.

Living God

*I make a decree, That in every dominion of my kingdom, men tremble and fear before the God of Daniel, for He is the **LIVING GOD** and steadfast forever and His kingdom, which will not be destroyed, and His dominion will be even to the end.* (Daniel 6:27)

- Hayah [2417], living (Aramaic)
- Elaha [426], God (Aramaic)

I AM Who I AM, I AM

*And God said to Moses, "**I AM WHO I AM!**" And He said, "Thus will you say to the children of Israel, **I AM** has sent me to you.* (Exodus 3:14)

- Ehyeh [1961], I am, I will be
- Asher [no #], who
- Ehyeh [1961], I am, I will be

Once we understand that He is the Living God, that He is alive and well, we need to develop our relationship in a more personal way. Eyeh can also be translated "I will be."

I AM

After these things the word of the LORD came to Abram in a vision, saying, "**Do not be in awe, Abram! I AM your Shield!** Your reward will be exceedingly great."* (Genesis 15:1)
- Anokhi [no Strong's #], I AM

The verb of being is not used in Hebrew, so the word AM is understood. Anokhi is a very powerful expression of God's protection. The "khi" suffix indicates purposeful, deliberate action by God. Anokhi is spoken by God more than one hundred times in Scripture, with this verse its first use.

I AM

And I will establish My covenant between Me and you and your seed after you in their generations for an everlasting covenant, to be a God to you, and to your seed after you. (Genesis 17:7)
- Ani [589], I AM

This is the common Hebrew word for I (am), Ani is used hundreds of times by God in Scripture. Ani is frequently used with verbs to express self, as in "I, *myself*, did.."

Jesus frequently referred to Himself by saying I AM, a statement of His Divinity that was clearly understood as such by His listeners.

My King and My God

*Listen to the sound of my cry, **MY KING AND MY GOD**, for I shall pray to You.* (Psalm 5:3)
- Malkhi [4428], my king
- VElohai [430], and my God

Each one of us must make Him my King and my God. Unless that personal headship is established, we have nothing, but once it is established we have everything!

The next name reinforces the concept that we are made in His image:

The Man

And David the king came and sat before the LORD* and said, Who am I, LORD* God, and what is my house, that You have brought me here? 17. And this was a small thing in Your eyes, O God, for You have spoken of your servant's house for a great while to come and have regarded me according to the estate of **THE MAN** *of high degree, LORD* God.* (1 Chronicles 17:16,17)
 - HaAdam [120], the man, mankind

God wants us to know Him and to know that we are made in His image. But even more, He desires a deeply personal, intimate relationship with each one of us.

Your Father

Do you requite the LORD* in this manner, O foolish and unwise people? Is not He **YOUR FATHER** *Who has bought you?! Has He not made you and established you?! Has He not made you and established* you *?!* (Deuteronomy 32:6)
 - Avi-kha [1], your father

He purchased our deliverance, our salvation with the blood of the Lamb, His Incarnate body.

My Father

But **I AM** *said, How will I put you among the children and give you a pleasant land, a goodly heritage of the hosts of nations? And I said, You will call Me,* **MY FATHER**, *and will not turn away from Me.* (Jeremiah 3:19)
 - Avi [1], my father

He wants each one of us to continually call Him "My Father."

Our Father, Our Redeemer, Eternal

Doubtless You are our Father, although Abraham was ignorant of us, and Israel does not acknowledge us. You, the LORD*, are **OUR FATHER, OUR REDEEMER**. *Your name is* **ETERNAL**. (Isaiah 63:16)

- Avinu [1], our father
- Go-elaynu [1350], our redeemer
- Me-olam [5769], eternal

In Jesus' day Pharisees frequently began prayers with Avinu, from Hosea 11:1 in which God calls "My Son" out of Egypt. All these uses of Father with a personal pronoun are from the Hebrew Scriptures because in Hebrew the personal pronoun is a suffix, part of the word Father. In Greek or English it takes a second word to say My or Your, but in the Hebrew language, the link is so secure that the Father has each of us as an integral part of His name as Father. Redeemer is listed here because the only redeemer in Hebrew is the kinsman redeemer, Our Heavenly Father in this verse.

Father

Therefore you must be praying in this way: our **FATHER**, *Who is in the heavens, Your name must at once be made holy.* (Matthew 6:9)

- Pater [3962], father

One Father

Have not all of us **ONE FATHER**?! *Has not one God created us?! Why do we deal treacherously, each man against his brother, by profaning the covenant of our fathers?* (Malachi 2:10)

- Av [1], father
- Ehad [259], one

God established the father-son relationship early. It is essential for us to have the understanding deep in our spirits that He is the ideal, the ultimate loving father. The B-D-B Hebrew-English Lexicon refers to this

Father relationship of God to His people. God is the one "Who constituted, controls, guides, and lovingly watches over it: Deuteronomy 32:6, Jeremiah 3:4,19; 31:9, Isaiah 63:16; 64:7, Malachi 1:6-2:10. And compare Exodus 4:22; 19:4, Deuteronomy 32:11, Hosea 11:1."

Those last verses also establish sonship. The Hebrew word for father, "Av," is transliterated into Greek, "abba," because there is no V sound in Greek. The Hebrew letter "vet" is transliterated into Greek as "B." Abba is also the Aramaic word for father. Abba is used in Mark 14:36, Romans 8:15, and Galatians 4:6. References to God as Father in the heavens, and as the Father of all men abound in the gospels and the epistles, as do references to our sonship. "Sonship," it should be noted, while grammatically masculine, does not exclude women from that relationship in the family of God. Just as men are included as members of the "Bride of Messiah," so women are included as part of the "sons of God." My favorite verse on sonship is *The one who conquers will inherit these things, and I shall be God to him and he will be a son to Me.* (Revelation 21:7)

The Lord wants even more than the father-son relationship with us, He wants to establish with us the oneness of spirit that can only come with marriage.

Your Husband
*For your Maker is **YOUR HUSBAND**! His name is the LORD* of Hosts and your Redeemer the Holy One of Israel. He will be called The God of the Whole Earth.* (Isaiah 54:5)
- Vo-alaikh [1166], your husband, married, lord

My Husband
And it will be at that Day, says the LORD, you will call Me Ishi, **MY HUSBAND**, and will no longer call Me Baali, **MY HUSBAND**.* (Hosea 2:16)
- Ishi [376], my husband
- Ba-ali [1166], my husband, lord, master

This reference shows us that the relationship with "Baali," meaning Husband as master and lord, has been replaced by that of the loving, equil husband-wife relationship. Ba-ali is the same word as Vo-alaik. Ishah meaning wife is first used in reference to Eve (Genesis 2:22,23,24). Ish means husband. God has declared the ultimate relationship in this utmost of intimacy, the husband-wife relationship. While Ish and Ishah can also be translated "man" and "woman," in Scripture these frequently refer to "husband" and "wife." In Genesis 2:23 Adam says, "She shall be called Wife (Ishah) because she has been taken out of Husband (Ish)."

Husband, Man
*And Jacob was left alone, and a **HUSBAND, MAN,** wrestled with him there until the breaking of the day.* (Genesis 32:25)
- Ish [376], husband, man

This is the first use of Ish (pronounced "eesh") in reference to God, expressing the intimate relationship He wants with each of us. Both the Hebrew and Greek words meaning to know (Yadah, Hebrew and G'nosco, Greek) connote this role of intimacy. God wants each of us to desire to really know Him and to seek His presence and His blessing as energetically and persistently as Jacob did that night. (*"Seek ye first the kingdom of God and His Righteousness.."* Matthew 6:33) God is truly the God of relationship. His greatest desire is to have an ongoing relationship with you.

I Will Make You a People of Covenant
Thus says the LORD, In an acceptable time I have answered You, and I have helped You in a day of salvation: and I shall preserve You and **I WILL MAKE YOU A PEOPLE OF COVENANT**, to establish the earth, to cause to Inherit the desolate heritages: (2 Cor. 6:2) 9. so You can say to the prisoners, **Go out!** To those who are in darkness, **Show yourselves!** They will feed by the roads and their pastures will be on all the high places.* (Isaiah 49:8,9)

- Etenkha [5414], and to give, hand over, grant, yield; to make
- Livrite [1285], for a covenant
- Am [5971], nation, people, folk, community

This is our Husband promising the covenant of marriage. The Living God, the King of the Universe, is in covenant relationship with each of us, and just as the Jewish wedding of Jesus' day was considered done at

the signing of the marriage contract, the marriage was not consummated until the home the bridegroom prepared was truly ready. He is preparing a place for us and when it is ready we will join Him at the marriage feast.

CHAPTER 5

God Is Love

Names Introduced in Chapter 5

Love	Agape
Gracious	Hanun
Compassionate	Rahum
He Will Not Forsake You	Lo Yarp'kha
Savior	Moshia
I Would Not Forget You	Anokhi Lo Eshkakhekh
I Taught, Teaching	Lamed, Lamed
Loving Kindness	Hasdi
Peace	Shalom
Sorry Over Calamity	Niham Al-Hara-ah
Who Forgives, Heals	HaSoleakh, HaRophe
Pardons Iniquity	No-se Avon
Passes Over Transgression	Ovair Al-Peshe
Erases Your Transgressions	Moheh F'shaykha
Will Not Remember Your Sins	Khatotaykh Lo Ezkor
Does Not Retain Anger Forever	Lo-Hakheziq La'ad Afo
Delights in Loving Kindness	Khafets Khesed
Who Heals	HaRof-e
Who Redeems	HaGo-el
Who Crowns With Loving Kindness & Compassion	HaM-atrekhi Hesed V'Rahamim
I Will Seek Out My Sheep	Avaker Tsoni

Benevolent	Haseed
Who Satisfies Old Age With Good	HaMasbiya Batov Edyekh
Renews Your Youth	CaNesher N'oray'khi
Executes Acts of Loving Kindness And Justice	Asah Ts'dakot OoMishpatim

This chapter is very, very rich, because our Father overflows with love for us. Each one of the words presented here is a base, a springboard for further, powerful study.

Love

*Beloved, we should love one another, because love is out of God, and everyone who loves has been begotten of God and does know the only God. 8. The one who does not love his brother does not know God, because God is **LOVE**..* (1 John 4:7,8)

    - Agape [26], love, esteem

*..for the Father Himself **LOVES** you, because you have loved Me and you have believed that I came from God.* (John 16:27)

    - Philei [5368], loves, phileo is the common spelling of this verb.

God is wholly love. His nature is summed up in love. God's many, many miracles demonstrate His love. His love for mankind in general was shown in His saving Noah. His love for Israel is illustrated in the miracles of Isaac's birth, and the later, countless miracles in the Exodus and in the Promised Land.

Gracious

*For that is his only covering, it is his clothing for his skin: in what will he sleep? And it will be, when he cries to Me, that I shall hear, for I AM **GRACIOUS**.* (Exodus 22:27)

    - Hanun [2587], gracious

Hanun is used twelve times in Scripture and is used only as an attribute of God. The root is kh-n-n [2603], meaning to show favor, to be gracious, merciful, compassionate. Since not one of us is worthy on his own merit, the salvation of each one of us is by His Grace.

Savior

Yet I AM the LORD* your God from the land of Egypt and you will know no god but Me, for there is no SAVIOR besides Me. (Hosea 13:4)

- Moshia [3467], savior

The Lord your God is the only Savior, with Jesus the name of His Earthly Incarnation. That is, God in the flesh, Who walked among us and dwells within us wherever we go. His love for each of us is what makes available His Grace and Mercy that set us free.

Compassionate, He Will Not Forsake You

for the LORD* your God is a COMPASSIONATE GOD, HE WILL NOT FORSAKE YOU or destroy you or forget the covenant of your fathers which He swore to them. (Deuteronomy 4:31)

- Rahum [7349], compassionate
- Yarp'kha [7503], abandon you, forsake you

Rahum is used thirteen times in Scripture, always in reference to God. The root, r-kh-m means to love. Rahum is the adjective form, which is generally translated "compassionate." In modern English compassionate is understood to mean "sympathetic" – a concept that falls far short of its rich Hebrew meaning. Here it is translated "merciful," but it would really be more accurate to say GOD IS LOVE. Yarp'kha is also used in Joshua 1:5; both of these scriptures were familiar to the author of Hebrews, who referred to them in Hebrews 13:5. The "You" not being abandoned is singular, speaking directly to each one of us.

I Will Not Forget You

*Can a woman forget her nursing child, so she would not have compassion on the son of her womb? Yes, they may forget, yet **I AM WILL NOT FORGET YOU.*** (Isaiah 49:15)
- Anokhi [no Strong's #], **I AM**
- Lo [3808], not
- Eshkakhekh [7911], to forget, forsake

The use of Anokhi, indicates that He is very purposeful in His determination to be your shield. No matter what happens, He will not ever forget you or forsake you. This you is singular, He is talking to you alone.

I Taught Them, Teaching

*And they have turned the back to Me and not the face, though **I TAUGHT THEM**, rising up early and **TEACHING** them, yet they have not listened to take correction.* (Jeremiah 32:33)
- Lamed [3925], (both Taught & Teaching) to learn and to teach, study, memorize

He has taught and is teaching each one of us, if only we will listen and obey. *..and I shall cut an everlasting covenant with them, that I shall not turn away from them, to do them good, but I shall put My respectful awe in their hearts so they will not depart from Me. 41. Yea, I shall rejoice over them to do them good and I shall plant them in this land assuredly with My whole heart and with My whole being.* (Jeremiah 32:40,41) His heart cry for each of us is so filled with His love that He wants us to accept Him and His teachings. In spite of our past mistakes and in spite of our present imperfections, He is pouring out His love and His teachings. Our part to return this love is to listen and to strive to obey, to make every effort to overcome our past and to continually improve, day by day inching closer to His state of perfection. *Therefore you must continually be imitators of God as beloved children 2. and you must walk constantly in love, just as also the Messiah loved us and gave Himself over on our behalf, an offering and a sacrifice to God for a fragrant aroma.* (Ephesians 5:1,2)

Loving Kindness

But I shall sing of Your power. Yes, I shall sing aloud of Your **LOVING KINDNESS** *in the morning, for You have been my defense and refuge in the day of my trouble.* (Psalm 59:17)
- Hasdi [2617], my loving kindness

The root is h-s-d, in eager zeal; desire that requires action as evidence of loving kindness.

Peace

Then Gideon built an altar there to the LORD and called it The LORD* **PEACE,** Shalom. To this day it is still in Afrah of the Abiezrite.* (Judges 6:24)
- Shalom [7965], completeness, soundness, welfare, peace

This peace is much more than an absence of conflict. It means peace with God, especially in covenant relation. It is used about two dozen times this way. It also means peace in your heart, regardless of the external circumstances. This same peace prompted Paul and Silas, in jail at Philippi, to sing the praises of God while they were chained in stocks. (Acts 16:24-40) Like them, we all can be set free by resting in this Peace! This peace also includes your whole welfare, every aspect of your life. (See also Isaiah 54:10, Numbers 25:12, Ezekiel 34:25, 37:26, Malachi 2:5.)

Sorry Over Calamity

And he prayed to the LORD and said, I pray you, LORD*, was this what I said, when I was still in my country? Therefore I fled before to Tarshish, for I **knew** that You were a gracious and compassionate God, slow to anger and of great loving kindness and **SORRY OVER CALAMITY.** *(Jonah 4:2)
- Niham [5162], to be sorry, regret, suffer grief
- Al [5291], over
- HaRa-ah [7451], evil, misery, distress, injury

Although Niham is sometimes translated "repent," "sorry" is correct. The root n-h-m [5162] means to be sorry, to console oneself. The Hebrew words Yatav and Shuv are used for repent. Yatav [3190] means to be good, to make a thing good, and in the imperative, to amend your ways. Shuv [7725] means to turn back, return.

Forgives, Heals

Who FORGIVES all your iniquities! Who HEALS all your diseases! (Psalm 103:3)
- HaSoelakh [5545], who pardons, forgives
- HaRof-e [7495], who cures, heals, remedies

It is His love for us that leads Him to forgive us. That He forgives ALL your iniquities has great significance because the Hebrew word translated iniquities means intentional sin that has been repented. The word 'you' is singular, so this promise is for each individual. His love also leads to His healing power, in this case diseases means any incidence of any illness, and the 'you' is singular.

Pardons Iniquity, Passes Over the Transgression, Does Not Retain His Anger Forever, Delights in Loving Kindness

Who is a God like You, Who PARDONS INIQUITY and PASSES OVER THE TRANSGRESSION of the remnant of His heritage?! HE DOES NOT RETAIN HIS ANGER FOREVER, because HE DIELIGHTS IN LOVING KINDNESS. (Micah 7:18)
- No-se [5375], to transfer, take, pardon, forgive
- Avon [5771], iniquity, guilt, intentional sin
- Ovair [5674], pass over, overlook
- Al-Pesha [6588], al [no #], means over; pasha means to transgress, rebel, willful sin that is committed with the intention of angering God
- Lo-Haheziq [2388], does not retain, hold
- La-ad [5703], forever
- Afo [639], his anger
- Hafets [2654], delight, wish, desire
- Hesed [2617], loving kindness

The iniquity that is pardoned is intentional sin! That is powerful! The transgression that is passed over is willful sin that is committed with the intention of angering God! How powerful His love must be in order for Him to be so forgiving. The remnant of His heritage is made up of those who have been faithful and **humble**. This comes from teachings about the remnant as seen in 1 Kings 19:18. Rabbi David Kimkhi, 12th & 13th century scholar wrote that the Hebrew Scriptures frequently use Humble to "denote the faithful minority in Israel who remained staunch throughout the national trials and did not yield to the pressure of the nations among whom they were scattered." There are about two dozen verses with this reference, but they are hidden in most English translations because the Hebrew word for humble, anav, is translated by different English words, as poor, meek, or lowly, in addition to humble.

Some of the verses where anav refers to the remnant are: *He will guide the humble in judgment and He will teach the humble His Way.* (Psalm 25:9) *But the humble will inherit the earth (Matt. 5:5) and will delight themselves in the abundance of Shalom.* (Psalm 37:11) *You caused judgment to be heard from heaven; the earth was awed and was still, 10, when God rose to judgment, to save all the humble of the earth. Selah.* (Psalm 76:9,10) *Surely He scorns the scorners, but He gives grace to the humble.* (Proverbs 3:34) *The humble also will increase their joy in the LORD*, and the humble among men will rejoice enthusiastically in the Holy One of Israel.* (Isaiah 29:19) *The Spirit of Adonai, the LORD*, is upon me, because the LORD* has anointed me to preach Good News to the humble. (Matt. 5:3) He has sent me to bind up the broken-hearted, to proclaim liberty to the captives, and opening of eyes (Isa. 42:7) for those who are bound,* (Isaiah 61:1) *Seek the LORD*, all you humble of the earth who have done His ordinance! Seek righteousness! Seek humility! It may be you will be hidden on the Day of the LORD's* anger,* (Zephaniah 2:3)

Often Anav is translated meek, but meek has a different connotation today, because meek now relates to low self-worth, a great lack of confidence. To be humble is to be without pride, but at the same time to have confidence, to know who you are in the Lord.

Erases Your Transgressions, Will Not Remember Your Sins

I AM, I AM He Who ERASES YOUR TRANSGRESSIONS for My own sake, and I WILL NOT REMEMBER YOUR SINS! (Isaiah 43:25)

- Moheh [4229], to erase, wipe, wipe out (off); blot out, efface
- F'sha-ekha [6586], to commit a crime, transgress
- Lo [3808], not
- Azkor [2142], to remember, recall, bear in mind
- Hatotekha [2403], your unintentional sin,

This passage is very powerful. God uses the word Anokhi in this verse for "I", which means that He is deliberately and determinedly forgiving and wiping away the sins. Moheh is in the present tense, showing that He is continuously forgiving, never ceasing. Fesha refers to rebellion, to sins that are committed with the intention of angering God. Ekha, the suffix, is the plural pronoun your, so this applies to all who walk in relationship with God.

Ezekiel 18:22 says, *All his transgressions that he has committed, they will not be mentioned against him. He will live in his acts of loving kindness that he has done.* The Hebrew word used for sin in this verse is fesha, sin committed to intentionally anger God, the worst of all possible sins. God even deletes those from His computer. Those sins were never committed!

There are numerous references in the New Testament that speak of reward. Revelation 2:21. *And I gave her time so that she could repent, but she does not want to repent from her idolatry. 22. Behold I am casting her and those who commit adultery with her into a bed in great torment, unless they would repent from her deeds. 23. And I will put her children to death in eternal death. And all the congregations will know that I AM the One Who examines minds and hearts,* (Ps 7:9, Pr 24:12, Jr

11:20, 17:10) and I will give to each one of you according to your Deeds. (Ps 62:12, Pr 24:12, Jr 17:10)

Revelation 20:13. *Then the sea gave up the dead that were in it and death and Hades gave up the dead, those in them, and each was judged according to his works.* We will be judged for what we do. All those who have repented and have given their hearts to God, even those sins committed willfully and even those committed to anger God will be forgiven. The things that have been done will however affect the reward, the heavenly assignment, for the former sinner.

Redeems, Crowns You With Loving Kindness and Compassion

Who REDEEMS your life from destruction! Who CROWNS YOU WITH LOVING KINDNESS AND COMPASSION! (Psalm 103:4)
- HaGo-el [1350], Who redeems
- HaM-atrekhi [5860], Who encircles, crowns, adorns
- Hesed [2817], loving kindness
- V'Rahamim [7356], and to love, pity, have compassion

The Kinsman Redeemer not only redeems you, He encircles, crowning you with loving kindness and compassion. He truly cares about you and feels the same pain you feel.

Does Not Favor Leaders

How much less to Him Who DOES NOT FAVOR LEADERS, or regard the rich more than the poor?! For they all are the work of His hands. (Job 34:19)
- Lo [3808], not
- Nasa [5375], to bear, pardon, endure
- Sar [8269], ruler, captain, chief, prince

Yes, He does encircle **you** with loving kindness and does not give more love to anyone because of position, or fame, or birth, or for any other reason. He loves you every bit as much as He loves any other person on the earth. There is no one whom God loves more than you.

I Will Seek Out My Sheep

*As a shepherd is seeking his flock on the day that he is among his sheep that are scattered, so will **I WILL SEEK OUT MY SHEEP** and will deliver them out of all places where they have been scattered on the cloudy and dark day.* (Ezekiel 34:12)
- Avaker [1239], to visit, attend, examine, review
- Tsoni [6629], my sheep

The word translated seek out has a primary meaning of examine and to visit. He does examine our hearts continually and He is with us all the time. He never leaves us. This verb is also translated "seek out" which He does when we feel alone, lost, and in need of comfort. He will seek you out and rescue you. See Chapter 10 for more on rescue.

Benevolent

Go and proclaim these words toward the north and say, Return, you backsliding Israel, says the LORD, and I shall not cause My anger to fall upon you, for I AM **BENEVOLENT**, says the LORD*, and I will not keep anger forever.* (Jeremiah 3:12)
- Haseed [2817], kind, benevolent

Haseed includes all the qualities of kindness and love. All the qualities of Haseed are brought to life in the Living God. No one English word can begin to capture the full meaning of this word. Truly He is **LOVE**, and He loves you more than you could imagine.

He will not bear a grudge against you, but is eager for you to repent so He can forgive you.

Satisfies Your Old Age With Good Things, Renews Your Youth

*Who **SATISFIES YOUR OLD AGE WITH GOOD THINGS**, so that **YOUR YOUTH IS RENEWED** like the eagle's!* (Psalm 103:5)

- HaMasbiya, [7646], satisfied, satiated, content, have abundance
- BaTov, [2896], with good things
- Edikh, [5716], your mouth, desire, old age

Edikh is difficult to translate into English. This verse speaks of material abundance and also eating wisely, both material food and spiritual food. We ought to take great care to eat foods the Bible advises and limit our spiritual intake to Scripturally correct things, rather than politically correct things.

- Tithadash [2318], to renew, renovate, regenerate
- CaNesher [5404], like the eagle
- N'oray'khi [5271], your youth

You are to stay youthful. Part of being youthful is openness, being receptive to new revelation by Our Heavenly Father, to supposedly new things like the dance, singing Psalms that are reflected on the wall, learning about the Jewish roots of Christianity and incorporating those into the local congregation. When you start to feel your age, remember that to restore your youth is a promise of God. Once again, the 'you' here is singular. The eagle, like every bird molts, shedding its feathers and growing new feathers. To renew our youth we are to shed the external things, then grow the eternal things as we grow spiritually, becoming more like Him. In eternal life we are always young in spirit and mature at the same time.

Executes Acts Of Loving Kindness and Justice
The LORD* EXECUTES ACTS OF LOVING KINDNESS AND JUSTICE for all that are oppressed. (Psalm 103:6)
- Asah [6213], execute, do, make
- Ts'dakot [6666], righteousness
- OoMishpatim [4941], and judgment
- Asah, executes

These verses from Psalm 103 flow together so naturally that they are all placed in this chapter. Also, they are all appropriate for they are the result of God's love.

God is grieved by the situations into which we get ourselves. Yet we must act and the action required is our repentance. Then God will remove our sin and bring about our deliverance, as He did at Nineveh. Also, He has given us authority over the enemy – an authority that, all too often, Christians fail to exercise.

CHAPTER 6

Authority

Names Introduced in Chapter 6

Most High God	El Elyon
King of Heavens	Melekh Shemaya
Possessor of Heavens and Earth	Koneh Shamayim VaArets
God of Heavens and Earth	Elah Shemya VeAr'a
God in the Heavens	Elohim BaShamayim
The Majesty	Tes Megalosunes
God of gods	Elohe HaElohim
Potentate	Dunastes
The King of the Kings	Ho Basileus ton Basileuonton
Lord of the Lords	Kurios ton Kurieuonton
Lord of the Lords	Adonai HaAdonim
Lord of Kings	Mare Malkhin
The King of the Nations	Ho Basileus ton Ethnon
My Lord	Adonai
The Judge	HaShaphet
Loves Justice	Ohev Mishpat
Ponders Hearts	Toven Livot
Examines Minds and Hearts	Eraunon Nefrous kai Kardias
Searches the Heart	Hokar Lev
Tests the Inward Parts	Boher K'layot
Rewarder	Misthapodotes
God of All the Earth	Elohe Kol-haArets

God of All the Kingdoms of the World	Elohim l'khol Maml'khot HaArets
Ruler in the Kingdom of Men	Shalit BeMalkhut Enasha
Executing Judgment	Aseh Mishpat
The Judge of All the Earth	HaShophet Kol-haArets
God of All Flesh	Elohi Kol-Basar
He Who Decrees	Bimhokek

How blessed we are to be children of the most loving Father of all eternity, and thus beneficiaries of His acts of love and grace. The One also is the most powerful force in creation and He uses this power and authority to make the way for us, to protect us, to heal us, and to provide for us. In this chapter we look at His authority. Some of these names, "King of Kings," "Lord of Lords" and the "Judge," for example, are also used as names for Jesus. Those included in this chapter, however, when taken in context, refer to the Father.

Most High God

And blessed be the **MOST HIGH GOD**, *Who has delivered your enemies into your hand. And he gave him tithes of all.* (Genesis 14:18)
- El [410], God (singular), El signifies power
- Elyon [5945], highest, most high

Elyon is used about twenty times as a name of God.

King of Heavens

Now I, Nebuchadnezzar, praise and extol and honor the **KING OF HEAVENS**, *all the works of Whom are truth, and His Ways judgment, and those who walk in pride He is able to abase.* (Daniel 4:34)
Melekh [4430], king
- Shamaya [8065], heavens (Aramaic)

Possessor of Heavens and Earth

And he blessed him and said, "Blessed be Abram of the Most High God, POSSESSOR OF HEAVEN AND EARTH. (Genesis 14:19)

- Koneh [7069], possess; here of God as originating, creating.
- Shamayim [8064], heavens
- VaArets [776], and the earth, (the planet), land, a country

God is far more than just a king. He created the universe, including each of us, and now possesses the universe. Although singular here in English, there is no singular for "heaven" in Hebrew; it is always plural, "heavens" in Hebrew. In Greek, however, the singular is sometimes used in reference to the sky, as in Matthew 16:2 " *..for the sky is red."* The Lord's Prayer (Matthew 6:9) literally reads *"..Our Father Who (is) in the Heavens."* Generally, the Greek is used in the plural.

There are seven Hebrew words used in Scripture to describe the heavens, so early rabbinic study cites seven levels of heaven. Paul spoke of the third heaven (2 Corinthians 12:2) and surely knew the rabbinic teaching of the seven levels. No matter how many heavens there are, He possesses and reigns as King over all, even as He possesses the earth.

God of Heavens and Earth

And thus they returned an answer saying, We are the servants of the God of Heaven and Earth, and build the House that was built these many Years ago, which a great king of Israel built and finished. (Ezra 5:11)

- Ela [426], God (Aramaic)
- Shemaya [8065], heavens (Aramaic)
- VeAr'a [772], and the earth (Aramaic)

God in the Heavens

..and said, LORD*, God of our fathers, are You not GOD IN THE HEAVENS? And You rule over all the kingdoms of the

nations? And in Your hand is power and might, so that no one is able to withstand You? (2 Chronicles 20:6)
- Elohim [430], God (plural)
- BaShamayim [8064], in the heavens

The Majesty
*But the main thing for those who are being addressed is that we have such a High Priest, Who has sat down on the right hand of the throne of **THE MAJESTY** in the Heavens,* (Hebrews 8:1)
- Tes Megalosunes [3172], the majesty

This word is used only in biblical and ecclesiastical writing, emphasizing the truly majestic nature of God.

God of gods
For the LORD your God is **GOD OF gods** and Lord of lords, (Rev. 19:16) a great, a mighty, and an awesome God, Who does not show favoritism or take a bribe.* (Deuteronomy 10:17)
- Elohe [410], God of
- Elohim [430], gods

He is supreme and far outranks the false gods who have no reality. The false gods could not be capitalized in this verse, even though the word gods is part of the name used here.

Potentate, The King of Kings, Lord of the Lords
*..which in His own time God will show, the blessed and only **POTENTATE, THE KING OF KINGS AND LORD OF THE LORDS** 16. the only One Who has immortality, unapproachable Light, Whom no one of mankind saw and no one is able to see: to Whom be honor and sovereignty forever, amen.* (1 Timothy 6:15)
- Dunastes [1413], potentate, powerful, sovereign
- Ho Basileus [935], leader of the people, prince, commander, king
- Ton Basileuonton [935], of the kings
- Kurios [2962], possessor or owner of, master, lord
- Ton Kurieuonton [2962], of the lords

The Lord of the Lords
For the LORD your God He is the God (Elohai) of Gods (Elohim), **THE LORD OF THE LORDS**, the Great, the Mighty, the Revered, Who shows no favor (literally, does not lift up faces) and takes no bribe.* (Deuteronomy 10:17)
- HaAdonai [113], the lord
- HaAdonim [113], the lords

Lord of Kings
*The king answered Daniel and said, Of truth your God is God of gods and **LORD OF KINGS** and Revealer of Secrets, since you were able to reveal the secret.* (Daniel 2:47)
- Mareh [4756], lord (Aramaic)
- Malkhin [4430], kings, kingdoms (Aramaic)

King of the Nations (Heathens)
*Who would not revere You, **KING OF THE NATIONS (HEATHENS)**? (Rev. 15:4) For to You only does it pertain, since among all the wise men of the nations and in all their kingdoms there is no one like You.* (Jeremiah 10:7)
- Melekh [4428], king
- HaGoyim [1471], the nations, heathens

Goyim can be translated either nations or heathens, and while nations is placed first here, heathens reads every bit as well.

The Greek equivalent carries the same relationship to heathen.

The King of the Nations (Heathens)
*And they sang the song of Moses, the servant of God, and the song of the Lamb, saying, Great and marvelous are Your works, God Almighty, righteous and true are Your ways, **THE KING OF THE NATIONS (HEATHENS)**.* (Revelation 15:3)
- Ho Basileus [935], the king
- Ton Ethnon [1484], of the nations, of the heathens

The Greek manuscripts have three variations for the word Ethnon, with Ethnon in the oldest and most reliable manuscripts.

It is thus most likely the correct word. It can be translated either as "nations" or as "heathens." Another early word used in place of the word translated heathens was aionon [165] meaning ages. Much later, around 1600 AD, the word hagion [40], meaning saints was substituted. We know and accept that He is King of all: King even over those who hate Him (heathens, ungodly nations), King of Eternity, of the Ages, and certainly King of the Saints, the unquestioned King of each believer.

My Lord
*And Abram said, "**MY LORD**, LORD*, what will You give me, seeing I go childless and the steward of my house is this Eliezer of Damascus?"* (Genesis 15:2)
- Adonai [113], my lord, master

This is the first use of Adonai in Scripture and each of us must make Him Lord of "my" life.

The Judge
I have not sinned against you, but you do me wrong to war against me. The LORD*, the Judge, be judge this day between the children of Israel and the children of Ammon. (Judges 11:27)
- HaShafet [8199], the judge, here to decide a controversy

Loves Justice
For I AM the LORD*. I love justice. I hate robbery with burnt offering and I shall direct their work in truth, and I shall cut an everlasting covenant with them. (Isaiah 61:8)
- Ohev [157], to love, desire
- Mishpat [4041], justice

The present tense of love shows that God forever pours out His love in justice. If others treat you unjustly, He will bring His justice to bear in the hereafter. You will be vindicated and recompensed.

Ponders Hearts

If you say, Behold, we did not know it. Does not He Who **PONDERS HEARTS** *consider it? And He Who keeps your soul, does He know it? And will not He render to every man according to his works? (Proverbs 24:12)*
- Tokhen [8505], examine, estimate, measure, ponder
- Libot [3820], hearts

Examines Minds and Hearts

And I will put her children to death in eternal death. And all the congregations will know that I AM the One Who **EXAMINES MINDS AND HEARTS,** (Revelation 2:23)
- Eraunon [2045], search, examine into
- Nefrous [3510], inmost thoughts, feelings
- Kardias [2588], hearts

Searches the Heart, Tests the Inward Parts

I AM, the LORD*, **SEARCHES THE HEART, TESTS THE INWARD PARTS,** *even to give to each man according to his ways, according to the fruit of his doings.* (Jeremiah 17:10)
- Hoker [2713], search
- Lev [3820], heart
- Boher [974], examine test, try
- K'layot [3629], inmost thoughts, feelings

Rewarder

..and without trusting it is impossible to please God: for it is necessary for the one who comes to God to believe that He is, that He does exist, then He becomes a **REWARDER** *to those who seek Him out.* (Hebrews 11:6)
- Misthapodotes [3406], rewarder

The primary meaning of this word is "the one who pays wages." In this instance it refers to God as the One Who rewards us, not only according to our deeds, but as our faith is accorded to us as righteousness. This is the only use of this word in Scripture although it is used several times in other ecclesiastical writings.

God of All the Earth
For your Maker is your Husband! His name is the LORD of Hosts and your Redeemer the Holy One of Israel. He will be called The **GOD OF ALL THE EARTH.*** (Isaiah 54:5)
- Elohai [430], God of (plural)
- Kol [3605], all
- HaArets [776], the earth

God of All the Kingdoms of the World
LORD of Hosts, God of Israel, Who dwells between the cherubim, You are the **GOD,** You alone, **OF ALL THE KINGDOMS OF THE WORLD,** You have made heaven and earth.* (Isaiah 37:16)
- Elohim [430], God
- L'khol [no Strong's #], of all
- Maml'khot [4437], the kingdoms
- HaArets [776], of the world

*For God so loved the **WORLD**.. He is Lord of all.*

Ruler in the Kingdom of Men
*And he was driven from the sons of men and his heart was made like the beasts, and his dwelling was with the wild donkeys. They fed him with grass like oxen, and his body was wet with the dew of heaven until he knew that the Most High God was **RULER IN THE KINGDOM OF MEN** and He appoints over it whomever He will.* (Daniel 5:21)
- Shalit [7990], having mastery, ruling (Aramaic)
- BeMalkhut [4437], in the reign, in the kingdom (Aramaic)
- Enasha [606], men (Aramaic)

God appointed Nebuchednezzar to carry off the nation of Judah and also removed Nebuchednezzar from office. We know that God raised Cyrus for the restoration of Judah. These historical facts demonstrate that God is truly all-powerful, able to place and remove presidents and kings.

The Judge of All the Earth
Far be it from You to do after this manner, to slay the righteous with the wicked and that the righteous should be like the wicked: far be that from You. Will not **THE JUDGE OF ALL THE EARTH** *do right?* (Genesis 18:25)
- HaShofat [8199], the judge, ruler
- Kol [3605], all
- HaArets [776], the earth, land, country

Executing Judgment
EXECUTING JUDGMENT *for the fatherless and widow, and loving the stranger, in giving him food and clothing. (Deuteronomy 10:18)*
- Oseh [6213], is executing
- Mishpat [4941], judgment

Unlike men, with God, Justice and Judgment are synonymous. His judgment is always perfect, always just.

God of All Flesh
Behold, I AM the LORD*, the **GOD OF ALL FLESH!** *Is there anything too hard for Me?* (Jeremiah 32:27)
- Elohai [430], God of
- Kol [3605], all
- Basar [1320], flesh, mankind

He Who Decrees
The chiefs dug the well, the nobles of the people sanctified it with the scepter, obeying **HE WHO DECREES**. *And from the wilderness they went to Mattanah* (Numbers 21:18)
- Hokek [2710], he who decrees, he who inscribes, lawgiver

Yes, He is the One Who Decrees. We are to be obedient, without questioning. We are to seek Him, to know Him, to abide in His presence.

He has all authority on earth and in the heavens. We have to truly recognize and accept His authority in every aspect of our lives. Until He is in fact Lord of our lives, we cannot move in the freedom or the anointing that God has designated for us.

CHAPTER 7

Power

Names Introduced in Chapter 7

God Almighty	El Shadai
Power	Dunameos
Who Removes Mountains	Hama'tik Harim
Who Shakes (the) Earth	Hamar'giz Erets
Consuming Fire	Esh Okhlah
Will Provide for Himself	Yireh-lo
Will Provide	Yireh
I Will Send You Grain, Wine & Oil	Sholeakh Lakhem Et-Hadagan V'Hatirosh V'Hayighar
Works All Things According to the Purpose of His Will	Tou ta Panta Energountos Kata ten Boulen Tou Thelematos
Who Commands the Sun	HaOmer LaHeres
Doing Wonders	Osch-Pele
My Miracle	Nisi
Sign	LeNes
Who Heals You	Rof'e-kha
My Strength	Heli

God not only has all authority in earth and in the heavens, He has all power. Although Satan was delegated authority on earth (John 12:31), our heavenly Father has given us authority and power over him.

(Matthew 28:18, Luke 24:49, Acts 1:8).

God Almighty

And when Abram was ninety-nine years old, the LORD appeared to bram, and said to him, "I AM **GOD ALMIGHTY!** Walk before Me and be innocent."* (Genesis 17:1)
- El [410], God (singular), El speaks of power Shadai [7706], of physical power, self-sufficient, omnipotent, mighty

The root of Shadai, sh-d-d [7703], means to deal violently. This is real physical power, and this statement includes the command to be innocent. The Hebrew word translated innocent is tamim [8549], sound, wholesome, unimpaired, innocent, having integrity. In verse 2 God tells Abram that He will make His covenant with him (a second covenant with him) and that He will give Abram many descendants. (Abram means "Exalted Father.") In verse 5 God changes Abram's name to "Abraham" (Chief of Multitude), certifying the promise that Abraham should have many descendants.

The Power

*And Jesus said, I AM. And you will see the Son of Man sitting at the right hand of **THE POWER**, and coming with the clouds of the sky.*
(Mark 14:62)
- Tes Dunameos [1411], of the power, strength, ability

Jesus here speaks of the Father as being **the** Power in the entire universe. Our Creator is the One Whom we must acknowledge in every way as Lord of our lives.

Who Removes Mountains
WHO REMOVES THE MOUNTAINS and they do not know it: He overturns them in His anger, (Job 9:5) See Matthew 17:20
- Hama'tik [6275], he who removes
- Harim [2022], the mountains

The mountains we create in our pride present far more numerous challenges to God than do the physical mountains of this earth.

Who Shakes the Earth
WHO SHAKES THE EARTH out of its place and its pillars tremble, (Job 9:6)
- Hamar'giz [7264], cause to quake, disquiet, enrage
- Erets [776], earth, land, country

Consuming Fire
For the LORD* your God is a CONSUMING FIRE, a jealous God. (Deuteronomy 4:22-24)
- Esh [784], fire
- Okhlah [398], devour, consume, as fire in judgment

His Consuming Fire is called out only after His chosen ones spurn Him for idols. Let us not ever be tempted by the things of this world so that we turn our backs on Him.

This God we serve has the power to move mountains, to cause earthquakes, and to consume our enemies. Beyond that, He has the power to create, the power and the love to provide whatever we need.

Will Provide for Himself
And Abraham said, "My son, GOD WILL SEE TO IT, PROVIDING A LAMB FOR HIMSELF." so they went, both of them together. (Genesis 22:8)
- Yir'eh-lo [7200], will provide for himself (will see to it)

Abraham walked in faith, knowing that God would honor His promise to make Abraham's seed more numerous than the dust of the earth (Genesis 13:16) and the stars of the heavens (Genesis 15:5).

Will Show Himself, Provide
And Abraham called the name of that place "The LORD Will See to it" as it is said to this day, "The LORD* **WILL SHOW HIMSLEF, PROVIDE**, on the mountain."* (Genesis 22:14)
- Yir'eh [7200], will provide, will see to it
- The root of Yir'eh is ra-ah [7200], which means to see.

This is similar to the idiom that we commonly use, saying that we will "see to" something, meaning that our listener can be sure that we will follow through and do whatever is needed.

I Will Send You Grain, Wine, and Oil
Yes, the LORD will answer and say to His people, Behold, **I WILL SEND YOU GRAIN, WINE, AND OIL** and you will be satisfied with it: and I shall no longer make you a reproach among the nations.* (Joel 2:19)
- Sholeakh [7971], will send
- Lakhem [No Strong's #], to you (plural)
- Et-Hadagan [1715], grain
- V'Hatirosh [8492], and wine
- V'Hayits'har [3323], and oil, particularly referring to Biblical scholars who "oil" one another as they explore interpretation of Scripture.

Oil is used to provide light, so it is a metaphor for revelation of Scripture.

Our Heavenly Father provides everything we need, from food, clothing and shelter, to revelation of His Spirit.

Works All Things According to the Purpose of His Will

In Whom our lot is cast, since we have been predestined according to the purpose of the One Who **WORKS ALL THINGS ACCORDING TO THE PURPOSE OF HIS WILL.** (Ephesians 1:11)

- Ta Panta [3956], all
- Energountos [1754], to work efficiently
- Kata [2596], according to
- Ten Boulen [1012], the counsel, purpose
- Tou Thelematos [2307], what one wishes or has determined shall be done (a purely Biblical word)
- Tou Autou [848], of himself

Sometimes we are uncomfortable in our temporary circumstances and we move in the flesh to make things happen. What is really needed in such times, however, is faith and a willingness to let God work things out.

Notice, too, that each of us is chosen by lot, not because we earned the honor. See Isaiah 28:16 in the Glossary of the One New Man Bible.

Who Commands the Sun

Who **COMMANDS THE SUN** *and it does not rise, and He seals up the stars.* (Job 9:7)

- HaOmer [559], the one speaking, commanding
- LaHeres [2775], to the sun

His power is so great that His spoken word has the ability to create (Genesis 1:3), or to make the sun stand still (Judges 14:18), or go back ten steps (2 Kings 20:9,10).

Shemesh is the common word for sun; Heres is the poetic word for sun.

Doing Wonders
Who is like You, LORD*, among the gods?! Who is like You, glorious in holiness, fearful in praises, doing wonders?! (Exodus 15:11)
- Oseh [6213], worker
- Pele [6382], wonder, miracle

My Miracle
And Moses built an altar and called the name of it Adonai-Nissi, The LORD is **MY MIRACLE**.* (Exodus 17:15)
- Nisi [5251], my miracle, standard, ensign, signal, sign

Nisi could be translated "sign" as in "signs and wonders." God is still performing signs and His people still call out to Him "show me a sign."

Moses named this altar in honor of the miraculous victory over the Amalekites, when Aaron and Hur held up Moses' arms and the staff of God, thus ensuring victory. Verse 16 *For he said, "Because the LORD* has sworn that the LORD* will have war with Amalek from generation to generation."* The hand upon the throne is the miracle.

Sign
*"And it shall be in that day when the Root of Jesse stands as a **SIGN** to peoples and nations shall seek Him and glory shall be His resting place."* (Isaiah 11:10)
- LeNes [5251], as a sign, standard, miracle
The Root of Jesse stands today as a "sign" to the world. All who are in Him must let Him show through us, that all will see Him when they look in our eyes, and in every work of our hands.

Who Heals You
If you will diligently hearken to the voice of the LORD* your God and will do that which is right in His sight and will give ear to His commandments and keep all His statutes, I shall put none

of these diseases upon you, I have brought upon the Egyptians, for I AM the LORD **WHO HEALS YOU*** (Exodus 15:26)
- Rof'e-kha [7495], heals you

Without question God wants each of us to call on Him for healing – before going to a doctor. His desire is to be our God of first resource, not our last resort. It takes self-discipline and practice for each of us to make prayer our immediate, natural reaction for first aid. But that quick, natural calling on Him is what is needed. The root of Rof'e-kha is r-f-a [7495], sometimes written Rapha in English.

My Strength
The LORD, my Lord, is **MY STRENGTH** and He will make my feet like deer's feet, and He will make me to walk on my high places.* (Habakkuk 3:19)
- Heli [2428], my strength, efficiency, wealth, army

This speaks of the extraordinary power of God, a strength that we can hardly imagine. This word is used the same way in Psalm 59:12. In Psalm 110:3 it is translated power in the KJV and Amplified, might in the NIV. This Strength, Might, Power, Efficiency, Wealth, Army is available to us. . . *you have not because you ask not.* (Jacob 4:2)

CHAPTER 8

Creator

Names Introduced in Chapter 8

Your Maker	Osekha
Who Stretched Forth the Heavens	Noteh Shamayim
Laid the Foundations of the Earth	Yosed Arets
Created the Heavens, Stretched Them Out	Bore HaShamayim, Notayhem
Spread Forth the Earth	Ro-ke HaArets
Who Made Pleiades and Orion	Oseh Khimah Ookhsil
Gives Breath to People,	Notem N'shama La-Am,
Spirit to Those Who Walk	Ruah LaHolkhim
Form Light & Creates Darkness,	Yotser Or Oovo-re Hoshekh
Makes Peace & Creates Chaos	Oseh Shalom Oovo-re Ra
Forms Mountains	Yotser Harim
Creates Winds	Oovo-re Ruah
Turns the Morning into Darkness	O-she Shahar Eifah
Maker of Heavens and Earth	Oseh Shamayim VaArets
Creator of the Ends of the Earth	Bo-re K'tsote HaArets
Creator of Israel	Bo-re Yisrael
Made Mankind	Na'aseh Adam
Male and Female He Created	Zakhar Oonkivah Bara
Built into a Woman	Yiven L'Ishah

Your Creator	Boraykha
Made You and Formed You	Osekha V'Yotserkha
Prepared Us	Y'khunenu
Our Potter	Yotsraynu
My Maker	Osy
Gives Songs in the Night	Noten Z'mirot Balay'lah
Teaches Us More Than the Beasts	Malfenu Mibahamot
Makes Us Wiser Than Birds	Me'of Y'khakmenu

Your Maker, Who Has Stretched Forth the Heavens, Laid the Foundations of the Earth

I AM, I AM He Who comforts you! Who are you, that you should revere a man who will die, and of the son of man who will be made like grass, 13. and forget the LORD* YOUR MAKER, WHO HAS STRETCHED FORTH THE HEAVENS, LAID THE FOUNDATIONS OF THE EARTH?! Have you feared continually every day because of the fury of the oppressor, as if he were ready to destroy? And where is the fury of the oppressor? (Isaiah 51:12,13)
- Osekha [6213], your maker
- Noteh [5186], spread, expand, stretch out
- Shamayim [8064], heavens
- V'yised [3245], and establish, set up, arrange, organize the foundation
- HaArets [776], the earth

Created the Heavens, Stretched Them Out, Spread Forth the Earth, Gives Breath to the People, Spirit to Those Who Walk

Thus says God, the LORD*, He Who CREATED THE HEAVENS and STRETCHED THEM OUT; He Who SPREAD FORTH THE EARTH, and that which comes from it; He Who GIVES BREATH TO THE PEOPLE on it and SPIRIT TO THOSE WHO WALK there. (Isaiah 42:5)
- Bo-re [1254], to create, form, shape, make
- HaShamayim [8064], the heavens
- Notayhem [5186], stretches them out, extends

- Ro-ke [7554], spread forth, stamp, stretch
- HaArets [776], the earth
- Noten [5414], gives
- N'shamah [5397], breath, spirit, life
- La-Am [5971], to the people
- Ru-ah [7307], spirit
- LaHolkhim [1980], to those who walk, go

The verbs is this verse, while translated in the past tense, are all in the Hebrew present. Even though the work of creation is finished, God's handiwork is still coming forth. The Spirit of God is still being given today. He is the same yesterday, today, and forever. (Psalm 102:27, Malachi 3:6, Hebrews 13:8)

Who Made Pleiades and Orion

*He **WHO MADE THE SEVEN STARS, PLEIADES AND ORION**, turns the shadow of death into the morning, makes the day dark with night, Who calls for the waters of the sea, and pours them out over the face of the earth, the LORD* is His name,* (Amos 5:8)
- Oseh [6213], made
- Khima [3598], Pleiades
- Kh'seel [3684], and Orion

The Pleiades are, in Greek mythology, the seven daughters of Atlas who were placed among the stars, or a large group of stars in the constellation Taurus. Orion is an equatorial constellation outlining a hunter with a belt and sword. The King of the Universe placed the stars where He wanted them and mankind has historically been fascinated by the patterns and found numerous familiar things outlined among them. Astrology is the study of these patterns with the assignments of meanings and interpretations to them. The men who visited the child Jesus in Bethlehem, bringing gold, frankincense, and myrrh were astrologers, not wise men or magi, which is Latin for astrologers.

Form Light and Creates Darkness, Make Peace and Creates Evil

> *I FORM THE LIGHT AND CREATE DARKNESS, MAKE PEACE AND CREATE CHAOS.* (Isaiah 45:7)
> - Yotser [3335], to create, manufacture, fashion, form, produce
> - Or [216], light, brightness, daylight
> - Oovo-re [1254], to create, form, shape, make, produce
> - Hosher [2822], dark, darkness, obscurity
> - O-seh [6213], to make, do, work, labor
> - Shalom [7965], peace, quiet, tranquility, safety; well-being, welfare, contentment, good condition.
> - Ra [7451], bad, chaos, anarchy

It is difficult to think of God as the creator of darkness and chaos, but in truth He is the creator of everything. There is nothing that He has not created. *"1.1. In the beginning was the Word, and the Word was with God, and the Word was God. 2. He was with God in the beginning. 3. All things came through Him, and there was not one thing that came into being without His participation."* (John 1:1-3) God made darkness because He knew we would need rest. He made evil because He wanted people who would love Him and serve in His will of their own volition. God did not want mindless robots, but He wanted true fellowship with His people, as He did for a season, walking in the garden with Adam and Eve. The free will we have gives us a challenge and makes life interesting for us all.

Forms Mountains, Creates Winds, Turns the Morning into Darkness

> *For, lo, He Who **FORMS THE MOUNTAINS** and **CREATES THE WIND** and declares to man what is His thought, Who **MAKES THE MORNING INTO DARKNESS** and treads on the high places of the earth, the LORD* God of Hosts is His name.* (Amos 4:13)
> - Yotser [3335], to create, manufacture, fashion, form, produce
> - Harim [2022], mountains
> - Vo-re [1254], to create, form, make, produce

- Rua_h [7307], wind, spirit
- O-seh [6213], to make, do, turn
- Eifah [5890], darkness, gloom, obscurity
- Sha_har [7837], dawn, break of day

It is significant that these verbs are present tense, because that means He is still forming mountains and creating winds today. See the next chapter, Defender, for "recounts to a person what were his deeds," and "tramples upon the heights of the earth,"

Made Heavens and the Earth
Our help is in the name of the LORD*, Who MADE HEAVENS AND THE EARTH. (Psalm 124:8)
- Oseh [6213], made
- Shamayim [8064], heavens
- VaArets [776], and the earth

The Creator of the Ends of the Earth
Have you not known? Have you not heard, the everlasting God, the LORD*, THE CREEATOR OF THE ENDS OF THE EARTH, does not faint nor is weary? There is no searching of His understanding. (Isaiah 40:28)
- Bo-re [1254], create, form, shape, make, produce
- K'tsote [7098], the limit of
- HaArets [776], the earth

The Creator of Israel
I AM the LORD*, your Holy One, THE CREATOR OF ISRAEL, your King. (Isaiah 43:15)
- Bo-re [1254], create, form, shape, make, produce
- Yisrael [3478], Israel, God perseveres or contends, or let God persevere, persist

Make Mankind
Then God said, "We will MAKE MANKIND in our image, after our likeness and have dominion over the fish of the sea, over the fowl of the air, over the cattle, over all the earth,

and over every creeping thing that creeps upon the earth."
(Genesis 1:26)
- Na'aseh [6213], will make
- Adam [120], mankind, man

He Created Male and Female
*So God created mankind in His own image; He created him in the image of God. **HE CREATED THEM MALE AND FEMALE.*** (Genesis 1:27)
- Zakhar [2145], male
- Oonkevah [5347], and female
- Bara [1254], to create, form, shape

Built Woman
*And He **BUILT** the rib, which the LORD* God had taken from man, **INTO A WOMAN** and brought her to the man.* (Genesis 2:22)
- Yiven [1129], to build, construct, establish, form
- L' [no Strong's #], to, into
- Ishah [802], woman, wife, female

The above three passages are very interesting, showing first that when God created the world, He made Adam out of material that He had already created. Asah, the word translated "made" expresses that. Next He explains that He created mankind, using the same word for create that He used in Genesis 1:1 when He created the Universe. Then in Chapter 2 He explains what He did Chapter 1:27 when He created male and female. Last of all in Genesis 2:22 He describes forming Adam's wife. God built Eve. The verb written here in the past tense has root letters of b-n-h. Another word pronounced BiNaH [Strong's #996] means to discern, to understand, so the rabbis teach that this is the reason that women are more spiritual and more sensitive than men. Using the words "Ish" and "Ishah" is significant, too. While those words can be translated "man" and "woman" they also mean "husband" and "wife," showing that Adam and Eve, husband and wife, truly were made for each other. There is another important point regarding their relationship in Genesis 2:18 when God says He will make a helper corresponding to

Adam. The word translated corresponding is K'neged, which has a root meaning of equal to and adequate for, so a wife is equal to her husband and adequate for any task that God assigns to the couple. Husband and wife are to be **one**, with both pulling equally on the yoke.

Your Creator

*Remember now **YOUR CREATOR** in the days of your youth, while the bad days do not come, or the years draw nigh, when you will say, I have no pleasure in them:* (Ecclesiastes 12:1)
- Boraykha [1254], create, form, shape, make, produce

Who Made You and Formed You

Thus says the LORD **WHO MADE YOU AND FORMED YOU** from the womb, Who will help you. **Do not be in awe! O Jacob, My servant, and you, Jeshurun, whom I have chosen!*** (Isaiah 44:2)
- Osekha [6213], to make you
- Yotserkha [3335], to create, form you

Yes, you have been made by the Lord, perfectly designed to perform His ministry here on this Earth, in this age. The kha suffix on each of the three verbs in those two verses are the pronouns your and you.

Fashion Us

*Did not He Who made me in the womb make him?! And did not One **FASHION US** in the womb?!* (Job 31:15)
- Y'khunenu [no Strong's #], prepared

Our Potter

But now, LORD, You are our Father. We are the clay and You are **OUR POTTER**, and we all are the work of Your hand.* (Isaiah 64:8)
- Yotsraynu [3335], our potter

We have to allow Him to shape us, to bring us into His ministry, not run on our own and build my ministry or our ministry.

My Maker, Who Gives Songs in the Night, Who Teaches Us More than the Beasts of the Earth, Makes Us Wiser than the Birds of the Sky

*But no one says, Where is God **MY MAKER, WHO GIVES SONGS IN THE NIGHT, 11. WHO TEACHES US MORE THAN THE BEASTS OF THE EARTH** and **MAKES US WISER THAN THE BIRDS OF THE SKY?*** (Job 35:10,11)
- Eloha [43], God
- Osy [6213], to make, do
- Noten [5414], to give
- Z'mirot [2176], songs
- Bala'ylah [3915], in the night
- Malfenu [502], to learn, teach, train, domesticate
- Mibahamot [929, 930], beast, cattle
- HaArets [778], the land, earth, country
- Me'of [5775], fowl, bird
- HaShamayim [8064], the sky, heavens
- Yhakmanu [2449], wiser

Our Creator crafted each of us, to be exactly as He intended each to be. The One Who is THE Creator, gives us songs and still inspires songs in the night. He is the One Who set mankind over not just the beasts of the earth, but also gave us stewardship of all we survey. With each of us having free will, it is our responsibility to take care of all He has placed in our charge.

CHAPTER 9

Defender

Names Introduced in Chapter 9

Lord of Hosts	Adon Tseva-ot
Man of War	Ish Milhamah
The Lord Will Fight for You	HaAdon (Y) Yilahem Lahem
He Will Wage War for You	Hanilham Lakhem
Who Will Defend His People	Yarayv Amo
I Will Deliver You	Oshia Etkhem
I Will Protect You	Etsrekha
Declares to a Person His Thought	Magid Mah Sekho
Treads on the High Places	Dorekh Al-Bamatei
He Who Goes Over Before You	Hu Ha-over
Who Goes Before You	Haholekh Lifnekhem
One Who Breaks Forth	Haporets
Guardian of Man	Notser Ha'Adam
Your Rear Guard	Oomasifkhem
Your Rear Guard	Ya-asfekha
Keeps Your Soul	Notser Nafsh'kha
Shield	Magen
Our Shield	Maginenu
God of Vengeance	El-Nekamot
Lord God of Vengeance	Adon El Nekamot

| He Takes Revenge Against His Foes | Nokem Litsaraiv |
| He Keeps Wrath Against His Enemies | Noter Le'Ovaiv |

God is our Defender, with an army on earth ready to move in our behalf. All too often we move in the flesh, denying His army the opportunity to accomplish His most perfect will. We need to have the faith and sensitivity that Elisha had: *And Elisha prayed and said, LORD*, now please, open his eyes so he can see. And the LORD* opened the eyes of the young man, and he saw and, there! The mountain was full of horses and chariots of fire all around Elisha.* (2 Kings 6:17)

Lord of Hosts
*And this man went up out of his city yearly to worship and to sacrifice to the **LORD* OF HOSTS** in Shiloh. And the two sons of Eli, Hophni and Phineas, the priests of the LORD*, were there.* (1 Samuel 1:3)
- YHVH [3068], Lord
- Tseva-ot [6635], army, war, warfare, hosts

The Lord of Hosts is all around us, with us every minute. We must open our spiritual eyes and flex our spiritual muscles. "Lord of Hosts" is used over two hundred times in the Bible to refer to God. That does not count the use of "host of angels" or "all the host of heavens," which are additional examples of His desire to defend us.

Man of War
The LORD is a **MAN OF WAR**! The LORD* is His name.* (Exodus 15:3)
- Ish [376], man, husband
- Milhamah [4421], battle, war

He is ready to defend you as a husband defends his wife, or as a father defends his children.

Will Fight for You

The LORD **WILL FIGHT FOR YOU**, and you will hold your peace.* (Exodus 14:14)
- Yilahem [3898], will fight, do battle
- Lakhem [no #], for you

This was spoken beside the Red Sea just after the Israelites saw the army of Pharaoh marching against them and the Israelites were afraid.

And when Pharaoh drew near, the children of Israel lifted up their eyes and, behold, the Egyptians marched after them, and they were greatly afraid, and the children of Israel cried out to the LORD*. 11. And they said to Moses, "Have you taken us away to die in the wilderness – because there were no graves in Egypt? Why have you dealt like this with us, to carry us forth out of Egypt? 12. Is this not the word that we spoke to you in Egypt saying, Let us alone, so we can serve the Egyptians? For it is better for us to serve the Egyptians, than that we should die in the wilderness." (Exodus 14:10-12)

Sadly, many in the Church today do not have the faith for spiritual warfare. It is just as necessary today as it was in Exodus to take the authority that we have been given, then stand in faith and watch our Heavenly Father battle for us.

He Will Wage War for You

You will not be in awe of them, for the LORD your God, **HE WILL WAGE WAR FOR YOU**.* (Deuteronomy 3:22)
- Hanilham [3898], will fight, wage war, do battle
- Lakhem [no #], for you

This is a different conjugation of the same verb translated "Fight for You." To wage war carries a much stronger message than to fight, because now He has sent His heavenly hosts, His amazing army. Be confident, **do not fear,** because the Lord, Your God, is with you and you can be sure He will go to battle for you.

Who Will Defend His People

Thus says your Lord, the LORD and your God **WHO WILL DEFEND HIS PEOPLE**, Behold, I have taken the cup of reeling even the dregs of the cup of My fury out of your hand! (Rev. 14:10; 15:7; 16:19) You will not drink it again,* (Isaiah 51:22)

- Yarayv [7378], to quarrel, fight, to plead for someone, defend
- Am, [5971], nation, people, community

Yes, He will defend our Godly nation as well as the nation of Israel, and those communities, such as churches, that obey and worship Him.

I Will Deliver You

And the LORD said to Gideon, **I WILL DELIVER YOU** by the three hundred men who lapped and deliver the Midianites into your hand. Let all the other people go, each man to his place.* (Judges 7:7)

- Oshia [3467], I will deliver
- Etkhem [no #], you

God has a number of ways of telling us to trust Him, of reminding us that He will fight our battles. When the Israelites were trapped by the fast charging army of Pharaoh by the Red Sea, the Lord said *"Fear not, stand still, and see the salvation of the Lord .."* (Exodus 14:13) Shortly after that Moses raised his staff and the Red Sea was divided so that all Israel was able to walk across on dry ground, then turn and watch the One True Living God dispatch Pharaoh's army by bringing the waters back over it.

Gideon had a different experience. The man whom God found at the wine press in order to keep his wheat hidden from the Midianites, went into battle unarmed, with only 300 men. The Midianites and the Amalekites covered the valley "like grasshoppers for multitude," but the Lord had caused them to flee from Gideon's 300 who were armed only with torches and trumpets!

God is saying to each one of us, "Know Me! Trust Me!"

I Will Protect You
Thus says the LORD, In an acceptable time I have answered you, and I have helped You in a day of salvation: and **I WILL PROTECT YOU** and make You a people of covenant, to establish the earth, to cause to Inherit the desolate heritages: (2 Cor. 6:2) 9. so You can say to the prisoners, **Go out!** To those who are in darkness, **Show yourselves!** They will feed by the roads and their pastures will be on all the high places.* (Isaiah 49:8,9)
> - Etsr'kha [5341], and to guard, keep, tend, preserve, protect you

This is true protection, promising to guard us from evil, to tend us, taking care of us in every situation. The word you is singular, so this applies to us collectively as a people and individually.

He Who Goes Over Before You
Understand therefore this day that the LORD your God is **HE WHO GOES OVER BEFORE YOU**. He will destroy them like a consuming fire, (Heb. 12:29) and He will bring them down before your face so you will drive them out and destroy them quickly, as the LORD* has said to you.* (Deuteronomy 9:3)
> - Hu [no #], he
> - Ha-over [5674], pass on before

That our God is a Consuming Fire should not cause us to tremble, but to rejoice! Let every believer be confident that He goes before each of us every step of the way, when we are in His perfect will, and that He prepares the way for us with His Consuming Fire!

Declares to a Person What is His Thought, Treads on the High Places of the Earth
*For, lo, He Who forms the mountains and creates the wind and **DECLARES TO A PERSON WHAT IS HIS THOUGHT**, Who makes the morning darkness and **TREADS ON THE***

HIGH PLACES OF THE EARTH, *the LORD* God of Hosts is His name.* (Amos 4:13)

- Magid [no Strong's #], herald, narrator, from Migad, to sweeten, give delight
- L'Adam [120], to a man, person, mankind
- Mah-Se<u>h</u>o [4100-7808], what-*were* his thoughts, deeds
- Dorekh [1869], to step, walk, go; to press, tread down, trample on
- Al-Bamati [5921-1116], on, upon-elevation, platform, high place
- Arets [776], earth, land

God tells you your past thoughts and deeds to lift your spirit! He does not keep track of repented sin. In Ezekiel 18:33 He forgets any sin He has forgiven. It is not in His computer, so it never happened! That is why the thoughts and deeds He recounts use a word with the root meaning, "to sweeten." The primary meaning of the word translated deeds is **thoughts**. As Paul wrote, *"For though we walk in the flesh we are not serving as soldiers according to the flesh, 4. for the weapons of our warfare are not fleshly but powerful in God for the tearing down of strongholds, tearing down reasonings 5. even every high thing being lifted up against the knowledge of God, and taking captive every thought in obedience to Messiah, 6. and being ready to punish every disobedience, when your obedience would be achieved."* (2 Corinthians 10:3-6) Jesus said, *"But I am saying to you that everyone who looks at a woman with desire for her has already committed adultery with her in his heart."* (Matthew 5:28) God knows your thoughts as well as your deeds, so it is critical to take captive every thought, to be truly transformed, becoming more like Him every day. God recounts your thoughts and deeds to lift your spirit. Satan recounts sins to pull you down. Take every thought captive and refuse to listen to Satan. See Sin, Forgiveness of, in the Glossary of The One New Man Bible.

To trample upon the high places is a metaphor for humbling the haughty. So those who are proud will get what is coming to them. Each of us is to be humble, as Moses was humble. *3. Now the man Moses was very humble, more than all the men on the face of the earth."* (Numbers 12:3) Although humble, Moses was definitely in charge, even arguing with God. Humility is a lack of pride, but not a lack of confidence.

Who Goes Before You

The LORD your God **WHO GOES BEFORE YOU,** He will fight for you (Exod. 14:14, Deut. 3:22), according to all that He did for you in Egypt before your eyes,* (**Deuteronomy** 1:30)
- Haholekh [3212], the one going
- Lifnekhem [6440], before you, in front of you

With God going before you, how can you fail? The key is to be in God's perfect will. If you are where He wants you to be when He wants you to be there, then you will know that He has gone ahead of you. Spend time with Him, so you will know Him. Only then can you be obedient. You will come to appreciate that it is not your plans that have any real merit, only His. When we walk with Him, He protects us.

One Who Breaks Forth

*The **ONE WHO BREAKS FORTH** has come up before them, they have broken forth and have passed through the gate and have gone out through it. (Gen. 28:14) And their king passed before them and the LORD* was at their head. (Micah 2:13)*
- Haporets [6555], the one who breaks, breaks through, demolishes, erupts, makes a breach, cracks, destroys

This power is to bring His people back to Israel as the previous verse in Micah says: *I shall surely assemble all of you, O Jacob. I shall surely gather the remnant of Israel. I shall put them together like the sheep of a sheepfold, like the flock in the midst of their fold: they will make great noise by reason of the multitude of men.* (Micah 2:12)

He will move mountains to bring His people to the Holy Land. He will move mountains in your life, too. He will break forth through the hurdles in your life to lead you in the way He would have you go, then acting as your rear guard as you go.

Guardian of Man

*I have sinned. What will I do for You, O You **GUARDIAN OF MAN?!** Why have You set me as a mark for You, so that I am a burden to myself?!* (Job 7:20)
- Notser [5341], to guard, keep, tend, protect
- HaAdam [120], the man, mankind

Notser is actually a verb, literally saying He is guarding you (singular) right now, right where you are. He is tending, nurturing you as He protects you.

HaAdam, literally "the man," can refer to all mankind, as well as to each one of us. God cares about you and for you.

Your Rear Guard

For you will not go out with haste, or go by flight, for the LORD will go before you, and the God of Israel will be **YOUR REAR GUARD.*** (Isaiah 52:12)
- Oomasifkhem [622], will be your Rear Guard

This "you" is singular! The King of the Universe is your personal Rear Guard!

Your Rear Guard

Then your light will break forth as the morning, and your health will spring forth speedily, and your righteousness will go before you. The Glory of the LORD will be **YOUR REAR GUARD.***" (Isaiah 58:8)
- Ya-asfekha [622], your rear guard

This "you" is plural, but His glory is enough to protect you and all of us!

Keeps Your Soul

*if you say, Behold, we did not know it. Does not He Who ponders the heart consider it? And He Who **KEEPS YOUR SOUL,** does*

He know it? And will not He render to every man according to his works? (Proverbs 24:12)
- Notser [5341], guard, keep, tend, preserve, protect
- Nafsh'kha [5315], your (singular) life, soul

Shield
After these things the word of the LORD came to Abram in a vision, saying, "**Do not be in awe, Abram! I AM your SHIELD! Your reward will be exceedingly great.**" (Genesis 15:1)*
- Magen [4043], shield

The root of Magen, g-n-n [1598] means to cover, surround, defend. Surely His desire is to protect us. Each of us needs to be aware that He has provided Himself as our Shield. The I AM in this verse is Anokhi, indicating His purposeful determination to be your shield.

Our Shield
Do not slay them, lest my people forget! Scatter them by Your power and bring them down, Lord **OUR SHIELD** (Psalm 59:11)
- Maginenu [4043], our shield

We must pray, claiming this Shield regularly. It can be powerful to protect those going into danger, to protect our loved ones daily, and to protect ourselves. He is with us. We have but to ask.

God of Vengeance, Lord God of Vengeance
O GOD OF VENGEANCE, O LORD GOD OF VENGEANCE, shine forth. (Psalm 94:1)El [410], God (singular), El speaks of power
- Nekamot [5360], vengeance
- YHVH [3968], LORD

Nekamot is used eleven times in reference to God's taking vengeance on the enemies of His people.

Takes Revenge Against His Foes, Keeps Wrath Against His Enemies

> *God is jealous and the LORD* takes revenge. The LORD* takes revenge and is furious. The LORD* will* **TAKE REVENGE AGAINST HIS ADVERSARIES** *and* **KEEPS WRATH AGAINST HIS ENEMIES.** (Nahum 1:2)
> - Nokem [5358], takes vengeance
> - Litsaraiv [6862], against his foes, adversaries
> - Noter [5201], he keeps, maintains
> - LeOvaiv [341], against enemies of God

LeOvaiv is used about a dozen times referring to the enemies of God. God wants you to know that He is your Defender and that He wants you to call on Him first when you have a need. He does not like to be your "God of Last Resort." God, the One Who created the universe, surely has all power. Each of us must grasp that truth and put in our spirits that His power is with us – to heal physically, to heal our inner hurts, to guide us daily, and to provide all our needs. These are some of our covenant rights. To receive those rights, all we need to do is fulfill our part of the covenant – to give God everything we have. The covenant is personal. Each believer must yield all things to God. That includes all the pride, all the fears (fear of men, fear of heights, fear of failure, fear of authority –all fears), all intellect, all possessions – everything belongs to Him. We must also give Him our time. He treasures personal time with each of us. I must leave the camp (world) and go to my tent, just as Moses did in Ex. 33:7-11. After I have done all these things, He makes His power available to me to minister to others, and to receive His blessings.

To keep this in perspective we must know that when persecution comes He is with us. If a believer is martyred, he knows that to die is gain (Philippians 1:21).

CHAPTER 10

Refuge

Names Introduced in Chapter 10

Our Refuge and Strength	Mahaseh V'Az
Refuge	Hahosim
My Strength	Hizki
My Rock	Sal'i
My Fortress	Metsudati
My Deliverer	Mefal'ti
My Rock	Tsuri
Horn of My Salvation	Keren Yish'i
My High Tower	Misgabi
Will Deliver	Yehoshia
Delivered Me	Tatsileni
Deliver You	Ohalets-kha
God of My Rock, My Refuge	Elohai Tsur Ekheseh-bo
Tower of Victories	Migdil Yeshuot
God My Savior	The-o Soteri Mou
Our Savior	Soteros Hemon
Your Savior	Moshi-e-kha
My Salvation	Li LiShu-ah
Rock of My Salvation	Tsur Yish'i
My Hiding Place	Sit'ri Satar

As we have seen, this God we serve goes before us and surrounds us with His hosts. He also provides places of refuge, where we can rest in His peace while He fights for us. These sanctuaries, these refuges are not places for permanent retirement but are to use for rest and recovery from times of battle. These periods might be very brief or quite extended, but the time is to be spent with Him (Isaiah 40:31).

Our Refuge and Strength

*God is **OUR REFUGE AND STRENGTH**, a very present help in trouble.* (Psalm 46:1)
- Lanu [no #], to us
- Mahaseh [4268], refuge, shelter
- V'Az [5797], and strength, might

Mahaseh is used about a dozen times referring to God, for truly His desire is for all of us to make Him our refuge. Jeremiah uses Mahaseh in Jeremiah 17:17, saying, "You are my Shelter." Understanding the root of Az, a-z-z, augments the meaning because it not only means to be strong and mighty, but also to prevail against. We are to be overcomers. Now!

Refuge

As for God, His Way is perfect. The word of the LORD is tried. He is a shield to all those who seek **REFUGE** in Him.* (2 Samuel 22:31)
- Hahosim [2620], to seek refuge

Seek and you shall find (Luke 11:9) is the key. He has provided the Refuge, but we must seek it in Him.

My Strength

..and he, David, said, I shall love You, LORD, **MY STRENGTH**.* (Psalm 18:2)
- Hiz'ki [2391], my strength

This is the only occurrence of this word in the Bible. The root is kh-z-k, which means to be or to grow firm, strong. It refers to our walk with Him, indicating that as we grow spiritually, He strengthens us.

My Rock, My Fortress, My Deliverer, My Rock, Horn of My Salvation, My High Tower

The LORD* is MY ROCK and MY FORTRESS and MY DELIVERER, my God, MY ROCK in Whom I shall trust; my Shield, the HORN OF MY SALVATION, and MY HIGH TOWER. (Psalm 18:2)

- Sal'i [5553], my crag, cliff: Sal'i is the word in Numbers 20:11, for the rock which Moses struck. The root is s-l-h, [no #], to split, here a reference to a cliff.
- Metsudati [4686], my fortress, stronghold, fastness
- Mefal'ti [6403], my deliverer: Mefal'ti is used about twenty times, speaking of God as our deliverer. The root p-l-t [6403], means to escape. He does have a way out.
- Tsuri [6697], my rocky wall, cliff: Tsur is used 33 times as a figure of God as support and defense of His people. The root ts-u-r [6696] means to confine, bind, besiege, enclose.
- Keren [7161], horn (symbol of strength)
- Yish'i [3468], my deliverance, rescue, salvation, safety, welfare Yish'i has the same root as Yeshua (Jesus), y-sh-a [3467] to deliver.
- Misgabi [4869], my secure height, retreat. Misgabi is used about twelve times as a reference to God's providing security.

This is one of the most powerful, most comforting verses in the Bible.

Will Deliver

And all this assembly will know that the LORD* does not save with sword and spear, for the battle is the LORD's* and He WILL DELIVER you into our hands. (1 Samuel 17:47)

- V'natan [5414], will give, deliver

The words in the above verse were David's as he ran to meet Goliath! That is the way we need to approach our Goliaths.

Have Delivered Me
*And Who brings me forth from my enemies. You also have lifted me up on high above those who rose up against me. You **HAVE DELIVERED ME** from the violent man.* (2 Samuel 22:49)
- Tatsileni [5337], deliver me, rescue me

This word is used in Psalm 39:8, *"**DELIVER ME** from my transgressions."* The root, n-ts-l [5337], means to snatch away, deliver from enemies, deliver from sin and guilt. Another word translated as "deliver" or "rescue" is Halats:

Deliver You
*And call upon Me in the day of trouble! I shall **DELIVER YOU**, and you will glorify Me.* (Psalm 50:15)
- Ohalets-kha [2502], deliver you, rescue, save

The "kha" suffix is second person, you, singular. He will rescue you!! The root is h-l-ts, meaning to draw off or out, withdraw. He will remove us from traps set by the enemy. This is the word used in Psalm 91:15, *.. I will Deliver him and honor him.*

There are four Hebrew words translated "deliverance;" each with a little different connotation:
M'falti, to escape
Yoshia, to deliver, gain victory
Tatsileni, to be delivered, rescued, to deliver from sin and guilt
O'halets, to rescue, deliver, save, to be drawn off or out, withdrawn

Notice that Yoshia, from the same Hebrew root as Yeshu, Jesus' name, means to gain victory. He intends for each of us to lead a victorious life.

God of My Rock, My Refuge

*The **GOD OF MY ROCK** in Him will I trust. He is my shield and the Horn of My Salvation, My High Tower and **MY REFUGE**; My Savior; You save me from violence.* (2 Samuel 22:3)
  - Elohe [430], God of
  - Tsuri [6697], my cliff (of security), my rocky wall
  - Eheseh-bo [2620], take refuge in him

Tower of Victories

*He is the **TOWER OF VICTORIES** for His king and shows loving kindness to His anointed, to David, and to his seed forevermore.*
(2 Samuel 22:51)
  - Migdil [4024], tower
  - Yishuot [3444], victories (B-D-B Hebrew-English Lexicon), deliverance

Yishuot is a form of Yeshua, Jesus' name.

God My Savior

*My very being magnifies the Lord, and my spirit rejoiced on account of **GOD MY SAVIOR**,* (Luke 1:47)
  - The-o [2316], God
  - To Soteri Mou [4990], my savior

This was part of Miriam's response to Elizabeth after arriving at Elizabeth's home when both were pregnant. Paul uses the same Greek word:

Our Savior

*Paul, an apostle of Messiah Jesus, according to a command of God **OUR SAVIOR** and Messiah Jesus, our Hope,* (1 Timothy 1:1)
  - Soteros [4990], savior
  - Hemon [2257], our

God the Father is called Savior again in 1 Timothy 2:3 & 4:10, Titus 3:4, Hosea 11:4, and in the following Hebrew verse, so both God in Heaven and the Incarnate God are Savior. See Chapter 3.

Your Savior

For I AM the LORD your God, the Holy One of Israel, **YOUR SAVIOR**. I gave Egypt for your ransom, Cush and Seba for you.* (Isaiah 43:3)
- Moshi-e-kha [3467], your (plural) savior, deliverer

This is a use of the root word y-sh-a.

My Salvation

*He also will be **MY SALVATION**, for a hypocrite will not come before Him.* (Job 13:16)
- Li [no Strong's #], for me, my
- LiShuah [3444], for salvation

God Himself is FOR your (singular) personal salvation. If God is for you, who can be against you? See Romans 8:31.

Rock of My Salvation

The LORD lives! Blessed be my Rock! And God is exalted! **ROCK OF MY SALVATION!*** (2 Samuel 22:47)
- Tsur [6697], rocky wall, cliff, God as support and defense of His people
- Yish'i [3468], deliverance, rescue, salvation, safety

Yish'i is also from the root y-sh-a, so it too has a wealth of meaning.

My Hiding Place

*You are **MY HIDING PLACE** (Ps. 32:7) and my Shield: I hope in Your word.* (Psalm 119:114)
- Sit'ri [5643], my covering, hiding place.
- Satar, [5641], is the root of Si't'ri and means to hide, conceal.

Surely, He is our Refuge, our Savior, our Deliverer, our Protector in every way. It is interesting and very significant that deliverance and salvation are so intertwined that both the Hebrew yasha and the Greek soter refer to deliverance as well as salvation. Christian translators have focused on the salvation that we receive by faith, but deliverance is available there as well. Deliverance, like salvation, must also be taken by faith. Failing to seek and take hold of deliverance after having received God's salvation parallels those tribes of Israel that did not take their land after God brought them into the Promised Land. (Joshua 18:2,3)

CHAPTER 11

All Knowing

Names Introduced in Chapter 11

Only Wise God	Mono Sofo Theo
Wise of Heart	Haham Levav
Mighty in Strength	Amits Ko-akh
He Who Knows	Ha-vode-a
Witness	Ed
My Witness, My Attester	Adi, Sahadi
Discerns the Righteous One	Bohen Tsadeek
Sees Innermost Thoughts and Feelings	Ro-eh H'layot V'Lev
God of Knowledge	El De-ot

Only Wise God

*..to the **ONLY WISE GOD**, through Y'shua Messiah, to Whom be the glory forever, amen..* (Romans 16:27)
- Mono [3441], only, alone
- Sofo [4680], wise, forming the best plans and using the best means for their execution
- Theo [2316], God, any deity

There are many gods, such as intellect, power, wealth, but only One God and only One Wise God. All wisdom is in Him.

Wise in Heart, Mighty in Strength

WISE IN HEART and MIGHTY IN STRENGTH. Who has hardened himself against Him and has remained sound, uninjured?! (Job 9:4)

- Hakham [2450], wise
- Levav [3824], inner man, mind, will, heart
- Amits [553], to be mighty
- Ko-akh [3581], strength, power

Ko-akh is used about three dozen times in speaking of the power of God. It refers to the power of creation, the power to rule, the power for deliverance, and the power of His works.

He Who Knows, Witness

..because they have committed villainy in Israel and have committed adultery with their neighbors' wives and have spoken lying words in My name, which I have not commanded them. Even I know and I AM HE WHO KNOWS and I am a WITNESS, says the LORD*.
(Jeremiah 29:23)

- Ha-vode-a [3045], he who knows
- Ed [5707], witness

This God we serve Knows and He is Witness to all we do. That is why Jesus could say that we are to go into our closet and shut the door when we pray (Matthew 6:6) and that we should keep it a secret from men when we fast, so God can reward in the open (Matthew 6:18).

A multitude of verses, both Hebrew Scriptures and New Testament reinforce this.

My Witness, My Attester

Also now, behold, MY WITNESS is in heaven, and MY ATTESTER is on high. (Job 16:19)

- Adi [5707], my witness
- Sahadi [7717], my witness, attester, observer

Adi and Sahadi are synonyms, which repetition is a common Hebrew way to express a superlative. Job is saying both that God is the greatest witness, that God does see and understand every act and even every thought that anyone has.

Discerns the Righteous One, Sees Innermost Thoughts and the Heart

But, the LORD* of Hosts, Who **DISCERNS THE RIGHTEOUS ONE** *and* **SEES THE INNERMOST THOUGHTS AND THE HEART**, *let me see Your vengeance on them, for to You have I opened my cause.* (Jeremiah 20:12)
- Bohen [974], to try, test, examine
- Tsadeek [6662], righteous one
- Ro-eh [7200], to see, look at, behold; to understand, conceive; choose, prefer
- Kh'layot [3629], innermost thoughts, literally kidney
- Lev [3820], heart

This verse has three Hebrew idioms, Bohen, literally to try or test, but used for discerning here; Kh'lavot, kidney, and Lev meaning heart. Kh'lavot and Lev are used often to refer to innermost thoughts and feelings.

Kh'lav was translated into Greek as splankhon, which in turn was inappropriately translated into English as inward parts or even bowels, or, more appropriately, as compassion. In the New Testament it should be translated as inward parts in Acts 1:18, but elsewhere as innermost thoughts or something similar. Both Discern and See are present tense, meaning that those actions are still going on.

God of Knowledge

Do not talk with excessive pride! Let proud talk not come out of your mouth, for the LORD* is a **GOD OF KNOWLEDGE** *and by Him actions are weighed.* (1 Samuel 2:3)
- El [410], God (singular), speaking of His power
- De-ot [1844], knowledge

He is in every sense the God of Knowledge. He knows not only what we do in the open and what we do in secret, but He has all wisdom. He gave through His Spirit the greatest book ever written. His Knowledge provides our every need.

CHAPTER 12

Abiding Presence

Names Introduced in Chapter 12

With You	Im'kha
My Presence	Panai
Face to Face	Panim el Panim
Presence	Mip'ne
Among You	Bekir'b'khem
Midst	Tavekh
I AM Will Be With You	Anochi Ehyeh Imkha
I AM With You	Ani Etkhem
I Have Walked	Hithalakhti

God's Abiding Presence with us is one of the His most precious attributes. He is with us always and His Abiding Presence is very real. These names are used many times, with His Presence woven through all Scripture. He is with us, but each of us has to walk with Him, knowing that His Presence is to shine through my eyes, be in everything I put my hand to. If I do not sense His Presence it is because I have separated myself from Him, because He will never leave or forsake me. (See p. 92)

With You
*And it happened at that time that Abimelech and Fikhol the chief captain of his army spoke to Abraham saying, God is **WITH YOU** in all that you do.* (Genesis 21:22)
- Imkha [no #], with you, singular

My Presence
And He said, "MY PRESENCE will go with you and I shall give you rest." (Exodus 33:14)
- Panai [6440], my face

Panai is used very, very often referring to the presence of God. It literally means "face" and the expression "faces to faces" is fairly common. Many times it is translated "before" – meaning in front of – God.

Face to Face
And Jacob called the name of the place Peniel, for "I have seen God FACE TO FACE and my life is preserved." (Genesis 32:30)
- Panim [6440], faces (this is the plural, literally faces to faces)
- Peniel means Face of God, referring to His presence with Jacob.

Presence
And they heard the sound of the LORD* God walking in the garden in the cool of the day, and Adam and his wife hid themselves from the PRESENCE of the LORD* God among the trees of the garden. (Genesis 3:8)
- Pne [6440], presence

Pne has the same meaning as Panim, used to indicate the Abiding Presence of the Lord throughout Hebrew scripture. It is used more than 150 times from Genesis through Deuteronomy.

Among You
And Joshua said, This is how you will know that the Living God is AMONG YOU, and He will without fail drive out from before you the Canaanite, the Hittite, the Hivite, the Perizzite, the Girgashite, the Amorite, and the Jebusite. (Joshua 3:10)
- Bekirbekhem [7130], midst, among, inward parts: the suffix ekhem means "you," plural.

Surely, He is Among us and has even more ways of expressing His Presence.

Midst
Therefore do not defile the land which you will inhabit, in IN THE MIDST of which I AM dwelling, for I the LORD* AM dwelling IN THE MIDST of the children of Israel. (Numbers 35:34)
- Betokhah [8432], in (the) midst (first Midst)
- Bitikh [8432], in (the) midst (second Midst)

The basic Hebrew word used here is "Tavekh" and is used twelve times in reference to the Divine Presence.

I AM Will Be With You
And he commanded Joshua the son of Nun and said, "Be strong! Be of good courage! For you will bring the children of Israel into the land which I swore to them and the I AM WILL BE WITH YOU."
(Deuteronomy 31:23)
- Anokhi [No Strong's #], I AM
- Eyeh [1961], will be
- Imkha [No Strong's #], with you (singular)

I AM With You
Then the LORD's* messenger Haggai spoke the LORD's* message to the people, saying, I AM WITH YOU: the word of the LORD*.
(Haggai 1:13)
- Ani [no #], I AM
- Etkhem [no #], with you

We surely do have His Abiding Presence and the assurance that He is in our Midst as we go to battle! The words in this chapter are used hundreds of times referring to His Presence.

I Have Walked
In all the places where I HAVE WALKED with all the children of Israel did I speak a word with any of the tribes of Israel, whom I commanded to feed My people Israel saying, Why have you not built Me a House of cedar? (2 Samuel 7:7)
- Hithalakhti [1980], I have walked, to walk or go

Our Heavenly Father walked with His people through their bondage in Egypt and their forty years in the wilderness. He is walking with you now, whether you are in a season of rest, with peace and comfort, or you are going through a very uncomfortable, painful season.

Trust Him. Know that He is with you. Each of us must make the decision to walk with God, as we can see in 1 Kings 11:33. *..because they have forsaken Me and have worshipped Ashtoreth the goddess of the Sidonians, Chemosh the god of Moab, and Milkom god of the children of Ammon and have not walked in My ways, to do what is right in My eyes, and to keep My statutes and My judgments, as did David his father.* It is our choice if we do not walk with God, because He will never leave us or forsake us. (Deuteronomy 4:31, 31:6,8, Joshua 1:5) It is possible for someone who wants to be in control to put Him in a locket to carry Him around, just opening the locket when trouble comes. The total commitment we should have puts Him in control 100% of the time. When anyone is determined to walk with God, he or she has God's assurance that He will be there too, every step of the way. Micah 6:8b says, *He has told you, O man, what is good.* **And what does the LORD* require of you, but to do justice, to love loving kindness, *(1 Cor. 13:3-7)* and to walk humbly in purity with your God?!** (See Introduction)

See page 97 for more on Humble.

For those of you who are familiar with the studies on the twelve names of God, the word "Shamah" is not included here because it is the Hebrew word for "there" and it is the name of the New Jerusalem in Ezekiel 48:35. He certainly will be there, but names in this chapter show that He is with us here and now!

CHAPTER 13

Help

Names Introduced in Chapter 13

My Help	B'ezri
Will hold Your Right Hand	Yahazik Y'minekha
I AM Helps You	Azartikha
I Have Helped You	Boethos

God is our Help and His Eyes roam over all the earth looking to show Himself strong to those whose hearts are blameless toward Him.
(2 Chronicles 16:9)

My Help

..and the name of the other was Eliezer, "For the God of my father was MY HELP and delivered me from the sword of Pharaoh." (Exodus 18:4)
- B'ezri [5828], my help

But do not be far from Me, LORD*! O My strength, hasten to MY HELP. (Psalm 22:20)
- Eyaluti [360], my help

Ezer is used about a dozen times referring to the Living God as "My Help!" Eyaluti is used only this one time. Remember that Yeshua (Jesus' name) is translated "Help" in 2 Samuel 10:11.

Will hold Your Right Hand, I AM Helps You

For I AM, the LORD your God, **WILL HOLD YOUR RIGHT HAND,** saying to you, **Do not be in awe! I AM HELPS YOU!** (Isaiah 41:13)*
- Mahazik [2388], take hold, grasp
- Y'minekha [3225], your right hand
- Ani [no #], I AM
- Azartikha [5826], helps you

The basic meaning of makhazik involves strength, so you must be confident that God's grasp is firm, that He will not drop you. He is speaking to us one at a time here since the word you is singular, when He says He has hold of you to help you.

Helper

*So that we may confidently say the Lord is a **HELPER** to me, and I will not be afraid, what will men do to me?* (Hebrews 13:6)
- Boethos [998], helper, helping

This is the only use of this particular word in the New Testament. Throughout all Scripture, however, we find God expressing – in almost countless ways – His desire that we lean totally on Him and trust completely in His ability and desire to move on our behalf. Remember Exodus 14:14, *"..the Lord your God will fight for you, and you be silent."* Let God rule in your life. Let Him perform a miracle for you. Let Him be your Helper. Trust God.

I Have Helped You

Thus says the LORD, In an acceptable time I have answered you, and **I HAVE HELPED YOU** in a day of salvation: and I will protect you and make you a people of covenant, to establish the earth, to cause to Inherit the desolate heritages: (2 Cor. 6:2) 9. so You can say to the prisoners, **Go out!** To those who are in darkness, **Show yourselves**! They will feed by the roads and their pastures will be on all the high places.* (Isaiah 49:8,9)
- Azartaykha [5826], to aid, help, assist

The King of the Universe is personally concerned about you, to assist you, to protect you, and to make all of us a people of covenant. In I Have Helped You, the pronoun you is singular to show His concern for each one of us.

CHAPTER 14

Name

Name to be Introduced in Chapter 14

Name	HaShem
LORD	YHVH
One	Ehad
Held in Awe	Nora

Name

*If you will not observe to do all the words of this Torah that are written in this scroll, so you will revere this glorious and awesome **NAME**, the LORD* your God,* (Deuteronomy 28:58)
- HaShem [8034], the name

This is a direct reference to YHVH, the personal name of our heavenly Father. In this verse God is talking of the curses due us if we are not obedient. But we must abide in the blessings through obedience according to the terms of the Covenant as stated in the first fourteen verses of this 28th chapter of Deuteronomy.

The LORD

*Therefore, behold, I shall at this time cause them to know, I shall cause them to know My hand and My might, and they will know that My name is **THE LORD***.* (Jeremiah 16:21)
- YHVH [3068], the LORD*

One

And the LORD will be King over all the earth. In that Day the LORD* will be One (John 17:11) and His name **ONE**.* (Zechariah 14:9)
- Ehad [250], one, single, first

Held in Awe

But cursed be the deceiver who has in his flock a male and vows and sacrifices a corrupt thing to the LORD, for I AM a great King, says the LORD* of Hosts and My name is **HELD IN AWE** among the nations.* (Malachi 1:14)
- Nora [3372], awe-inspiring

The root of nora is ya-re. The root means to revere, to be in awe of His Name is One, His Name is Awesome. We are to call Him the Lord God, the King of the Universe, and many other names that are appropriate. Whatever we do, we are to call Him and praise Him continually.

CHAPTER 15

Yah

Names Introduced in Chapter 15

Yah	Yah
My Strength	Azi
Song	Zimrat

Yah, My Strength, Song

> *YAH* is *MY STRENGTH, SONG* and melody for He has become my salvation. This is my God and I shall praise Him; the God of my father and I will exalt Him! (Exodus 15:2)
> - Yah [3050], the first syllable of God's personal name
> - Azi [5797], my strength, might
> - Zimrat [2176], melody, song (including instruments) in praise of God

Yah is used more than fifty times: twice in Exodus, four times in Isaiah, the other times in Psalms.

Each of us must say, "He is My Strength". Zimrat is used only three times in Scripture – here, in Psalm 118:14 and in Isaiah 12:2.

CHAPTER 16

Light

Names Introduced in Chapter 16

Father of Lights	Tou Patros Ton Photon
My Light	Ori
My Lamp	Neri
Sun	Shemesh

Father of Lights

*Every good gift and every perfect gift is from above, being sent down by the **FATHER OF LIGHTS**, with Whom there is not one change or shadow variation.* (James 1:17)
- Tou Patros [3962], The Father
- Ton Photon [5457], Of Lights

My Light

Since the LORD is **MY LIGHT** and my salvation – whom should I hold in awe?! The LORD* is the strength of my life – of whom should I be in terror?!* (Psalm 27:1)
- Ori [216], my light

My Lamp

*For You are **MY LAMP**, LORD*, and the LORD* will lighten my darkness.* (2 Samuel 22:29)
- Neri [5216], my lamp, prosperity, happiness, delight

The oil that fuels the lamp provides the illumination of Scripture to bring life, new revelation to God's Word.

Spending time daily with Him in His Word allows His Spirit to open our hearts and minds so that He can bring new meaning to each individual who is open to His thoughts. He is our Light and our Salvation, our Lamp, Prosperity, Happiness, Delight.

Sun

For the LORD God is a **SUN** and shield: the LORD* will give grace and glory! No good thing will He withhold from those who walk uprightly.* (Psalm 84:12)
- Shemesh [8121], sun

Sun He not only created the sun, He is the Sun to us, providing light and bringing all good things to us, a shield for our protection. *But to you who revere My name, the **SUN** of Acts of Loving Kindness will rise with healing in His wings and you will go out and prosper like fattening calves in the stall.* (Malachi 3:20) This is Chapter 4:2 in some English translations of Malachi.)

This is a picture of our Loving God daily giving us from His bounty, with food, healing, whatever is needed. Acts of Loving Kindness is the translation of the Hebrew Ts'dakah, and Wings speak of intimacy with Him. See Prayer Shawl in Glossary of the One New Man Bible.

CHAPTER 17

Truth

Name Introduced in Chapter 17

God of Truth	Emet

God of Truth
> *Into Your hand I commit My spirit. (Luke 23:46) You have redeemed me, LORD* **GOD OF TRUTH.*** (Psalm 31:5)
>> - Emet [571], firmness, truth
>> - Elohe [430], God of

CHAPTER 18

Portion and Inheritance

Names Introduced in Chapter 18

Your Portion	Helk'kha
Your Inheritance	Nahalat'kha
Portion of Jacob	Helek Yaakov

Your Portion, Your Inheritance

And the LORD* spoke to Aaron, "You will have no inheritance in their land, nor will you have any portion among them. I AM **YOUR PORTION** *and* **YOUR INHERITANCE** *among the children of Israel.* (Numbers 18:20)
- Helk'kha [2506], your portion, tract, territory
- Nahalat'kha [5159], your possession, property, inheritance

The Lord is speaking to Aaron concerning all the Levites who had no land to inherit. The Lord is the provider for all the priesthood, all ministry workers. We are to be a kingdom of priests, knowing the Lord as our provider, our healer, our deliverer. That does not mean to lie around, waiting for others to take care of our needs. It means we are to occupy, to use our God-given talents for income, but to do so in God's plan for each life, each of us being sensitive to the Spirit, not being slack, but being open to His plan for each life.

Portion of Jacob

> The **PORTION OF JACOB** is not like them, for He is the One
> Who Forms all things and Israel is the tribe of His inheritance:
> the LORD* of Hosts is His name. (Jeremiah 51:19)
>> - Helek [2506], portion, tract, territory
>> - Yaakov [3290], Jacob, one following closely

The root of Yaakov is a-k-v [6117], meaning to follow at the
heel, succeed, bring consequence on, i.e. reward or punish.
"Former" here means Creator, the One Who Forms.

God is absolutely our Portion and our Inheritance. We are to
trust totally in Him, rest in His support, and not look to our own
devices and our wealth for security.

CHAPTER 19

Object of Our Praise

Names Introduced in Chapter 19

Worthy to be Praised	Mehulal
Exalted	Gebah
The God of Glory	Ho Theos tcs Doxes
The God of Glory	El HaKavod
King of Glory	Melekh HaKavod
Majestic Glory	Megaloprepous Doxes

From Chapter 14 that "He is my Song!" That could be said of Him just as well here.

Worthy to be Praised

I shall call on the LORD, Who is **WORTHY TO BE PRAISED**. So will I be saved from my enemies.* (2 Samuel 22:4)
- Mehulal [1984], to be praised, worthy of praise

Exalted

..but the LORD of Hosts will be **EXALTED** in judgment, and God Who is Holy will be sanctified by acts of loving kindness by people.* (Isaiah 5:16; See also Isaiah 55:9)
- Gebah [1361], high, exalted

God of Glory

*And he (Stephen) said, "Men, brothers and fathers, you must listen. The **GOD OF GLORY** (Ps 29:3) was seen by our father*

Abraham while he was in Mesopotamia before he dwelt in Haran,.." (Acts 7:2)
- Ho Theos [2316], the God
- Tes Doxes [1391], of the glory

Here Doxes is used like the Hebrew Kavod, speaking of the Shekinah light of God. Shekinah means dwelling, referring to the presence of God, not directly to the light, but where He is there is Light!

The God of Glory

The voice of the LORD* is over the waters. **THE GOD OF GLORY** *thunders: the LORD* is upon many waters.* (Psalm 29:3)
- El [410], God (singular), El speaks of power
- HaKavod [3519], the abundance, honor, glory

The root of Kavod, k-v-d [3513], means to be honored (the exact Meaning depends on the conjugation). However, He is to be honored at all times and above all else.

King of Glory

Lift up your heads, O you gates and be lifted up, you everlasting doors, and the **KING OF GLORY** *will come in.* (Psalm 24:7)
- Melekh [4428], king
- HaKavod [3519], the abundance, honor, glory

The Greek words Humneo and Humnos have been transliterated into English as "Hymn," referring to singing praises to God. The Greek word Psalm has basically the same meaning, but also implies musical accompaniment. The Hebrew name of the book of Psalms is Tehilim, meaning Praises.

Majestic Glory

For then He took honor and glory from Father God when such a unique voice announced to Him by the **MAJESTIC GLORY**, *'This is My Son, My Beloved, with Whom I take delight,'* (2 Peter 1:17)

- Megaloprepous [3169], magnificent, splendid, full of majesty, majestic
- Doxes [1391], praise, honor, glory

Verse 18 of 2 Peter 1st Chapter tells us The Majestic Glory spoke to Peter, Jacob, and John on the Holy Mountain, the Mountain of Transfiguration, Matthew 17:5. *While he was still speaking, behold a radiant cloud overshadowed them, and there was a voice from the cloud saying, 'This is My beloved Son, with Whom I have been well pleased: you must habitually listen to Him.'*

All the Glory is His! All praise is His! He alone is worthy of praise, and we are to have no other gods before Him. That includes sports, TV, work, possessions. He is our Inheritance! To put any other god before Him serves to repudiate Him, to totally deny Him!

CHAPTER 20

Holy

Names Introduced in Chapter 20

The Holy God	HaElohim HaKadosh
The Holy One	Tou Hagiou
Holy One	Kadosh
Sanctifies You	Mekadoshekhem
Holy One of Israel	Kadosh Yisrael
Holy Ones	Kedoshim
Blameless	Tamim

The One True God is the only one Holy in His own right and the only One capable of making any one of us holy.

Holy God
And the men of Beit Shemesh said, Who is able to stand before the LORD, the **HOLY GOD?** And to whom will it go up from us?* (1 Samuel 6:20)
- HaKadosh [6918], sacred, holy, separated from human infirmity, impurity, and sin
- HaElohim [430], the God (majestic plural)

Beth-Shemesh was the Israeli city to which the Philistine lords returned the ark. The men of the city are asking to whom they should send the ark.

The root of Kadosh, k-d-sh [6942] means to be set apart, consecrated. When we are set apart by the blood of the Lamb we are new creations (2 Corinthians 5:17). We are not to return to our old ways once we are dead to sin (Romans 6:2,4,6,7, et al.).

The Holy One

*And you have an anointing from **THE HOLY ONE** and you know all things.* (1 John 2:20)
- Tou Hagiou [40], revered, worthy of veneration, set apart for God.

Holy One

*God came from Teman and the **HOLY ONE** from Mount-Paran, Selah. His glory covered the heavens, and the earth was full of His praise.* (Habakkuk 3:3)
- Kadosh [6918], sacred, holy, separated from human infirmity, impurity, and sin

Sanctifies You

Speak also to the children of Israel saying, Verily you will keep My Sabbaths for a sign between Me and you throughout your generations, so you will know that I AM the LORD Who **SANCTIFIES YOU**.* (Exodus 31:13)
- Mekadoshekhem [6918], sanctifies you

This is the One Who separates us from human infirmity, impurity, and sin.

Holy One of Israel

*Whom have you reproached and blasphemed? And against Whom have you raised your voice and lifted up your eyes on high? Even against the **HOLY ONE OF ISRAEL**.* (2 Kings 19:22)
- Kedosh [6918], sacred, holy (as above)
- Yisrael [3478], Israel, perseveres with God

Holy Ones

Reverence of the LORD is the beginning of wisdom, and the knowledge of the **HOLY ONES** is understanding.* (Proverbs 9:10)

- Kedoshim (plural of kedosh) [6918], holy ones

The plural, Ones, refers to the complexity of God. As we grow in knowledge of God in all His attributes, we grow in understanding of His desires and His plan.

Blameless

*As for God, His Way is **BLAMELESS**, perfect. The word of the LORD* is tried. He is a shield to all those who seek refuge in Him.* (2 Samuel 22:31)

- Tamim [8549], complete, sound, entire, innocent

We are never perfected while we dwell in these mortal bodies. But thank God, He does not see our sin when He looks at us, but instead sees His Son, the Messiah, the only Incarnate One Who achieved this state on earth and dwells in us. He is the only One worthy to be called the Lamb of God (John 1:29).

CHAPTER 21

Righteous

Names Introduced in Chapter 21

Righteous	Tsadik
Habitation of Righteousness	Neveh-Tsedek
Way of the Lord	Derekh HaAdon
Way of the Lord	Ten Hodon tou Kuriou

The Hebrew root word for Tsadik is ts-d-k, to be just, to be righteous. This is an action verb, indicating that we are required to do something – to act in certain ways.

God sets us apart in holiness by our repentant, circumcised hearts (Deuteronomy 10:16) and by the blood of the Lamb. To be righteous we must walk daily in obedience to the Father, as Abraham did when he took Isaac to Mt. Moriah (Genesis 21:1-10, Hebrews 11:17). For this reason the "Way" is included here.

Serving God according to His righteousness is a walk, a total commitment, a new way of life.

The Hebrew word ts'dakah, acts of loving kindness, is from the same root as tsadik. A sin of omission is as serious as a sin of commission (Remember the commandment to love your neighbor as yourself, Leviticus 19:18). While action is required, it must be done in the right spirit because we are justified by grace. *(Holy Spirit) Whom He poured out richly upon us through Jesus Messiah our Savior, 7. so that since we have been made righteous by the grace of that One, we would become heirs according to the hope of eternal life.* (Titus 3:6,7)

The English word "justified" is from the Latin word iustifico, spelled justifico in English letters, "to be righteous," meaning to be just, to be righteous.

Righteous

Whereupon the princes of Israel and the king humbled themselves and they said, the LORD* is RIGHTEOUS. (2 Chronicles 12:6)
- Tsadik [6662], righteous

After Alexander the Great conquered Israel in 332 BC, many of the wealthy and powerful Israelis started going to Greek theater and games, instead of to synagogue. They learned to speak Greek and studied little of Scripture, holding only to the books of Genesis through Deuteronomy, and not much of the teachings in those books. These people were called Hellenists, meaning Greek, and referred to themselves as the Tsadik. Tsadik was written in Greek as Sadducee. They were self-righteous, not Godly.

Habitation of Righteousness

All who found them have devoured them, and their adversaries said, We are not guilty because they have sinned against the LORD*, the HABITATION OF RIGHTEOUSNESS, the LORD*, the hope of their fathers. (Jeremiah 50:7)
- Neveh [5116], dwelling, abiding
- Tsedek [6664], rightness, righteousness

Neveh is used only one other time in scripture, in Psalm 68:13. Tsedek is the noun form and Tsadik the adjective. The root word is ts-d-k [6663], meaning to be just, to do justice, to be righteous.

Way of the Lord

*For I know him, that he will command his children and his household after him and they will keep the **WAY OF THE LORD**, to do acts of loving kindness and judgment, so the LORD* may bring upon Abraham that which He has spoken of him.* (Genesis 18:19)
- Derek [1870], way, road, distance, journey, manner
- YHWH [3050], the LORD

Derek is used about sixty times in the Hebrew scriptures referring to obedience to His commandments. "Journey" is a good translation, since moving – acting in obedience – is a necessary prerequisite to receiving and being made righteous by Grace.

Way of the Lord

*He was teaching the **WAY OF THE LORD** and being fervent in the spirit. He was speaking and teaching accurately the things about Y'shua, although he knew only the immersion of John:* (Acts 18:25)
- Ten Hodon [3598], the way, road, street, highway
- Tou Kuriou [2962], the lord, supreme controller, owner, master

The Way of the Lord requires a walk with Him. John wrote about walking in the light (1 John 1:7) and that is just what we have to do. He has not saved us just to sit back. Rather, we are saved for a purpose – to take up the great commission with zeal and to show God's love to others.

CHAPTER 22

Jealous

Name Introduced in Chapter 22

Jealous	Kana

God makes it very clear to us that He is to be the Lord of our entire lives, that we are not to put anything or anyone before Him.

Jealous

Mark well what I AM commanding you this day! See for yourself! I am expelling before you the Amorite, the Canaanite, the Hittite, the Perizzite, the Hivite, and the Jebusite. 12. 1 Take heed for yourself, that you do not cut a covenant with the inhabitants of the land where you are going, lest it be for a snare among you, 13. 2 but you will destroy their altars, break their images and cut down their groves, 14. 3 for you will worship no other god: for the LORD*, Whose name is JEALOUS, is a jealous God. (Exodus 34:11-14)

    - Kana [7067], jealous, ardor, zeal

Kana is used only in reference to God, and only on four other occasions, all in Exodus and Deuteronomy. The root is k-n-a [7065], to be jealous, zealous. Actually, Zealous is a better translation than jealous, because what the Lord is looking for is zeal for the Godly things and for righteousness, as Phineas was zealous for righteousness when he slew the Israelite man who brought a Midianite woman into the Tent of Meeting, Numbers 25:7,8. For his zeal Phineas was elevated to Priesthood and given an everlasting Covenant of Peace.

CHAPTER 23

Anger

Name Introduced in Chapter 23

Anger	Af

It is evident that, in order to walk in God's perfect will, it is absolutely essential to give 100% to Him, to do His Word, to obey every commandment. We must not, then, make covenants or other strong alliances with unbelievers, whether in business, by marriage, or socially. If we do form any of those alliances, this is what we can expect:

Anger

*Neither will you make marriages with them! You will not give your daughter to his son, nor will you take his daughter for your son. 4. For they will turn away your son from following Me so they may serve other gods, so the **ANGER** of the LORD* will be kindled against you and destroy you suddenly.* (Deuteronomy 7:3,4)

- Af [639], nostril, nose, face, anger

Notice that to incur the Anger of the Lord we have to go off and serve other gods, to turn our backs on Him. Avoiding close alliances with the unbeliever helps shield us – and our children – from this peril.

The LORD is **slow to anger** and great in power, but will not at all acquit the guilty. The LORD* has His way in the whirlwind, the dust of His feet are in the storm and the clouds.* (Nahum 1:3)

We should be eternally grateful that He is slow to Anger.

*For His **ANGER** lasts but for a moment, His favor is for a lifetime. Weeping may endure for a night, but a ringing cry of joyful praise comes in the morning.* (Psalm 30:6)

Not only is He slow to Anger, but He also gets over it quickly. In the same translation Micah 7:18 ends with:

*Who is a God like You, Who pardons iniquity and passes over, forgiving, the transgression of the remnant of His heritage?! **He does not retain His anger forever,** because He delights in loving kindness.* These verses from Nahum, Psalms, and Micah bring out the true nature of our God, that He is loving above all else. Although we can provoke His Anger, the Anger is slow in coming and quick in going.

CHAPTER 24

Eternal

Names Introduced in Chapter 24

Eternal King, Immortal, Invisible	Basilei ton Aionon, Aftharto, Aortato
Eternal God	El Olam
Ancient of Days	Atik Yomin
Who Is Who Was and Who Is Coming	Ho On kai ho en ho Erchomenos
Endures Forever	L'Olam

The Living God, Who by speaking created the heavens and the earth and all living creatures, is the God of all eternity.

Eternal King, Immortal, Invisible

*Now to the **ETERNAL KING, IMMORTAL, INVISIBLE**, the Only God, be honor and glory forever and ever, amen.* (1 Timothy 1:17)
- Basilei [935], king. leader of the people, prince
- Ton Aionon [166], without beginning or end, that which has always been and always will be
- Aftharto [862], immortal, uncorrupted, not liable to corruption or decay, imperishable
- Aorto [517], invisible, unseen

Eternal God

And Abraham planted a grove in Beer-Sheba, and there he called on the name of the LORD, **ETERNAL GOD**.* (Genesis 21:33)
- El [410], God
- Olam [5769], eternal, everlasting, long duration, antiquity

Ancient of Days

*I watched till thrones were cast down and the **ANCIENT OF DAYS** sat, whose garment was white as snow, and the hair of His head like pure wool. (Rev. 1:14; 20:4) His throne was like the fiery flame, his wheels like burning fire.* (Daniel 7:9)
- Atik [6268], advanced, aged
- Yomin [3118], days (Aramaic)

Who Is and Who Was and Who Is Coming

*John to the seven churches in Asia: Grace to you and peace from the **WHO IS, WHO WAS AND WHO IS COMING**, and from the Seven Spirits which are before His throne.* (Revelation 1:4)
- Ho [no #], one who
- On [5607], is
- Kai [no #], and
- Ho [no #], who
- En [2258], was
- Ho [no #], who
- Erchomenos [2046], is coming

Endures Forever

O give thanks to the LORD! For He is good, for His loving kindness **ENDURES FOREVER**.* (Psalm 136:16)
- L'Olam [5769], endures, lasts, is forever

The One Who accompanied His people through the wilderness for forty years, the Living God, is forever.

His love for each of us is as great today as it was for each of the children of Israel as He led them through the wilderness and as in 2 Samuel 7:7, *In all the places where **I have walked with all the children of Israel** did I speak a word with any of the tribes of Israel, whom I commanded to feed My people Israel saying, Why have you not built Me a House of cedar?* When you are in a wilderness experience you can count on Him to be there with you, walking every step of the way, no matter how long it takes. His Loving Kindness surely does Endure Forever. His Loving Kindness is translated sometimes as Mercy, but the Hebrew word is Khesed. See the chapter on Love for more on Khesed, which has no appropriate English translation.

Not only is He Eternal, but He also has made His eternal life available to all mankind. Jesus said *everyone who believes in Him would have eternal life.* (John 3:15). Eternity is a concept that is really not understandable because we move in a very finite world. When we study History, we generally think in terms of a few hundred years. A few thousand years is Ancient History. Eternity is thousands of billions of years. Eternity has no end, yet we are promised Eternal Life by the Eternal God.

CHAPTER 25

God of Israel

Names Introduced in Chapter 25

God of Israel	Elohe Yisrael
God of the Armies of Israel	Elohe Maarekhot Yisrael
God of Your Father	Elohe Avikha
God of Abraham	Elohe Avraham
God of Isaac	Elohe Yitskhak
God of Jacob	Elohe Yaakov
God of the Hebrews	Elohe HaIvriim
God of Jerusalem	Eleh Yerushlam
King of Jacob	Melekh Yaakov
Eminence of Israel	Natsah Yisrael
Mighty One of Israel	Avir Yisrael
King in Jeshurun	Melekh B'shurun

God persistently stresses that there is only one Promised Land, and one Chosen People. His covenant is eternal and it is being fulfilled right before our eyes. It is awesome to live in these times, where we see Israel being restored as a nation – where we see so much of His promise to Israel being literally fulfilled. We see also that Exodus II has already started. God has attached Himself to Israel until the end of this world!

We must let Paul's words lodge in our spirits:
Romans 11:16. *And if the first fruits is holy, the whole batch is also: and if the root is holy, the branches are also. 17. But*

*if some of the branches were broken off, and you,4 since you are a wild olive, were yourself grafted into them, then you would be a participant for yourself of the richness of the root of the olive tree. 18. Stop boasting of the branches: but, if you do boast, you do not support the root, but the root supports you. 19. Therefore you will say, 'Branches were broken off so that I could be grafted in.' 20. Just so: they were broken off by unbelief, but you have stood by faith. Do not be proud, but you must continually fear for yourself: 21. for if God did not spare the natural branches, **neither** will He in any way spare you. 22. You must now see the goodness and severity of God: on the one hand severity upon those who fell, but on the other hand goodness of God upon you, if you would remain in the goodness, otherwise you would be cut off. 23. And even these, if they would not remain in unbelief, they will be grafted in: for God is able to graft them in again. 24. For if you were cut off from the naturally wild olive tree and contrary to nature you were grafted into the cultivated olive tree, how much more will these natural branches be grafted into their own cultivated olive tree..* (Romans 11:16-24)

Christians are grafted into the only cultivated olive tree, and that is Israel.

God of Israel

And he erected an altar there, and called it El, **GOD OF ISRAEL.** (Genesis 33:20)
- Elohe [430], God of
- Yisrael [3478], Israel, God perseveres or contends, or let God persevere, Persist

God of Israel is written two hundred one times in the Hebrew Scriptures.

God of the Armies of Israel

Then David said to the Philistine, You come to me with a sword, with a spear, and with a shield, but I come to you in the name of

the LORD of Hosts, the **GOD OF THE ARMIES OF ISRAEL** Whom you have defied.* (1 Samuel 17:45)
- Elohe [430], God of
- Maarekhot [4634], armies
- Yisrael [3478], Israel, God perseveres or contends

God of Your Father, God of Abraham, God of Isaac, God of Jacob

*Moreover He said, "I AM the **GOD OF YOUR FATHER, GOD OF ABRAHAM, GOD OF ISAAC, AND GOD OF JACOB.**" (Matt. 22:32, Acts 3:13) And Moses hid his face, for he was afraid to look upon God.* (Exodus 3:6, see verse 16)
- Elohe [430], God of
- Avikha [1], your father
- Avraham [85], Abraham, chief of multitude
- Yitskhak [3327], Isaac, he laughs
- Yaakov [3290], Jacob, one closely following

The root of Yaakov is a-k-v, [6117], meaning to follow at the heel, to succeed, bring consequence on, i.e. reward or punish.

God of the Hebrews

And they will heed your voice and you will come, you and the elders of Israel, to the king of Egypt and you will say to him, 'The LORD **GOD OF THE HEBREWS** has met with us and now let us go, we beseech you, three days' journey into the wilderness, so we can sacrifice to the LORD* our God.'* (Exodus 3:18)
- Elohe [430], God of
- HaIvriim [5680], the Hebrews

God of the Hebrews is used six times, all in the Book of Exodus.

God of Jerusalem

*The vessels also that are given to you for the service of the House of your God, deliver those before the **GOD OF JERUSALEM.*** (Ezra 7:19)
- Elah [426], God of (Aramaic)
- Yerushlam [3390], Jerusalem (Aramaic spelling)

King of Jacob

Produce your cause, says the LORD. Bring forth your strong reasons, says the **KING OF JACOB**.* (Isaiah 41:21)
- Melekh [4428], king
- Yaakov [3290], Jacob, to follow at the heel

It is significant that God called Himself "King of Jacob" long after the nation of Israel had been carried off to Babylon. He was still their King – and still is their King. It is also significant that God used "Jacob" instead of "Israel". The name Jacob is used many times in Scripture, even after his name was changed to Israel, the only biblical character whose name was changed by God for whom this is true. Once Abram, Sarai, and Saul were given new names, these older names were never used again. After his name was changed to Joshua (Numbers 13:16), Joshua was only referred to one time by his former name, Hoshea, in Deuteronomy 32:44. Jacob's zeal and persistence were precious to God. That may well be why Jacob was the prophet chosen to introduce us to Shiloh, Messiah, Yeshua, the Shepherd and the Stone.

Eminence of Israel

*And also the **EMINENCE OF ISRAEL** will not lie or repent, for He is not a man that He should be sorry.* (1 Samuel 15:29)
- Natsah [5331], eminence, enduring, everlastingness, perpetuity
- Yisrael [3478], Israel, God perseveres, contends

This is a statement of his supreme authority and His eternal nature, all tied to Israel. Thank God that He made a way for us to be grafted in!

Mighty One of Israel

Therefore says the Lord, the LORD of Hosts, the **MIGHTY ONE OF ISRAEL**, Ah, I shall ease Myself of My adversaries and avenge Myself of My enemies.* (Isaiah 1:24)
- Avir [46], strong, mighty, valiant, courageous
- Yisrael [3478], Israel, God perseveres, contends

Avir is used six times in Scripture, each time as a description of God. He is always strong, mighty, valiant, and courageous as He watches over Israel to defend it and prepare it for the times to come.

King in Jeshurun

*And he was **KING IN JESHURUN** when the heads of the people and the tribes of Israel were gathered together.* (Deuteronomy 33:5)

- Melekh [4428], king
- ViYeshurun [3484], over straightness, righteousness, equity, uprightness, honesty, fairness, integrity, straightforwardness, sincerity, honesty of purpose

The Hebrew root is y-sh-r, meaning straight, righteous, upright. The Jewish scholar Sforno wrote hundreds of years ago "Once Israel declared its eternal loyalty to the Torah (Deuteronomy 33:3-4), God became 'King of Jeshurun,' because it is only among those who grasp and diligently involve themselves in the study of Torah that God is truly King."

CHAPTER 26

AMEN

Name Introduced in Chapter 26

Amen	Amen

Amen

Blessed be the LORD* God of Israel from everlasting to everlasting, and let all the people say, AMEN. HalleluYah! (Psalm 106:48)
- Amen [543]

Although universally thought to mean Truth or So Be It, that is not correct. Truth in Hebrew is Emet. So Be It is a translation from the Greek Genoito. The Latin Vulgate does not translate Amen, but just writes it with English letters, which is why the word Amen appears in English bibles, since the first English translations were made from Latin. There is no definition or translation because Amen is not a Hebrew word, although it is spoken and is used many times is Scripture. Amen is an acrostic meaning **"El Melekh Ne'eman"**, **"God is a Faithful King"**. So, when you say Amen, You are saying our Faithful God will see to it! It will be done!

AMEN!

CONCLUSION

How do you summarize God? This book is filled with descriptions from the Word of God of His love, His caring, His defending us, delivering us, of His presence. At best, a book can only hint at all the blessings that God desires for us. It can only hint at the power and authority that He has throughout the universe. All that He is, is far beyond the capacities of our imaginations, so we must receive from Him by faith, not by sight. (2 Corinthians 5:7)

A good summary of The King of the Universe is in Exodus 34:6,7 *And the LORD* passed by before him and proclaimed, "The LORD*, the LORD* God, merciful and gracious, patient, and abundant in loving kindness and truth, 7. keeping loving kindness for thousands, forgiving iniquity, transgression, and sin,...*

Without faith we have nothing from God. He is not an intellectual exercise to be puzzled out and thus apprehended. Rather, He is real: He is alive, and must be experienced. Only by standing in faith and relying totally on Him can we receive any of the characteristics described in this volume. He is not just the source of our hope and health and miracles, He **is** our **hope**, our **healer**, our **miracle**. If you open your heart, commit 100% to Him, then you can receive all that He offers. He is the God of relationship. His greatest desire is for each of us to truly know Him as Husband. Only then can each one walk with Him as we make our individual ways through all of life's challenges. All the names and notes contained in this book, while they represent a great time of research, do not mark the end of this study. These are little more than the beginning of a never ending relationship. The time spent on this project has been a blessing to me and I know that more names are to be revealed.

Even more than that, there is much greater depth in many, many of the names of God that can now be pursued because the time once spent on this project will be available for new things.

Recognizing that this book merely scratches the surface, my hope is that it will be a springboard for thousands of pastors and teachers and saints to follow up where this leaves off, gleaning all the potential from different names.

The character of God as revealed by these names is one of such caring, and of deep love and affection for all who make Him Lord of their lives. In the third chapter of Jeremiah, I could feel His sadness as He spoke of the idolatry, and I could feel His longing as He lamented that His own did not call Him "MY FATHER." The feeling I had was that He wanted each one of His children to climb up in his lap to say "MY FATHER."

Praise God that His lap is big enough for all of us at the same time! Even more than the most loving earthly father, He wants to defend us, protect us, provide refuge for us, heal us, and provide for us in every way. He is truly our Miracle Worker, yet He asks only that we honor Him, forsaking all other gods, and that we love our neighbor as ourselves (Deuteronomy 6:5, Leviticus 19:18, Matthew 22:37-39).

Those of you wishing to research these names further need just a few books to do it. The most essential ones are a Hebrew Lexicon and a Greek Lexicon. The lexicons are essential because they give the changes in meanings for the different cases of nouns and adjectives, and also for the different conjugations, tenses, and voices of each verb. Next are a Hebrew Concordance and a Greek Concordance. There are no books that this author knows of with Hebrew and Greek combined in one volume that are as complete and as accurate as these. Some of the books that are combinations (both Hebrew and Greek) are incorrect in the Hebrew roots, or add meanings that are questionable. An Interlinear Bible with literal translation and Strong's Concordance numbers over each Hebrew and each Greek word is also very helpful.

CONCLUSION

Basic books are listed here:

1. The New Brown-Driver-Briggs-Gesenius Hebrew English Lexicon, Francis Brown, D.D.,D.Litt.,

2. The New Englishman's Hebrew Concordance, Wigram,

3. The New Thayer's Greek-English Lexicon, J. H. Thayer,

4. The New Englishman's Greek Concordance and Lexicon, Wigram-Green

5. The Interlinear Bible, Hebrew-Greek-English, Jay P. Green, Sr.

All the above are published by Hendrickson Publishing, Peabody, Massachusetts and can be ordered from any bookstore. They are also available from Amazon.

The above books were recommended by The Center for Judaic Christian Studies of Dayton, Ohio, and Jerusalem. Each of those books is coded with Strong's Concordance numbers.

INDEX

Name	Page	Scripture
Captain of the Army	44	Joshua 5:14
Comforter	10	John 14:15,16
Comforter of Israel	62	Luke 2:25
Comforting the Lowly, The One	10	2 Corinthians 7:5,6
Coming, The One	54	Hebrews 10:37
Compassionate	81	Deuteronomy 4:31
Consuming Fire	103	Deuteronomy 4:22-24
Cornerstone	51	I Peter 2:6,7
Cornerstone, Head	51	I Peter 2:6,7
Cornerstone, Precious	51	Isaiah 28:16
Counsel	15	Psalm 73:24
Counselor	45	Isaiah 9:5
Covenant People, I Will Make	77	Isaiah 49:8
Created the Heavens	110	Isaiah 42:5
Created He, Male and Female	114	Genesis 1:27
Creates Chaos	112	Isaiah 45:7
Creates Darkness	112	Isaiah 45:7
Creates Winds	112	Amos 4:13
Creator of Israel	113	Isaiah 43:15
Creator of the Ends of the Earth	113	Isaiah 40:28
Creator, Your	115	Ecclesiastes 12:1
Crowns You With Love	87	Psalm 103:4
Dayspring	61	Luke 1:78
Daystar	37	2 Peter 1:19
Decrees, He Who	99	Numbers 21:18
Defend His People, Who Will	120	Isaiah 51:22
Delights in Loving Kindness	84	Micah 7:18
Deliver Me	130	2 Samuel 22:49
Deliver You	120	Judges 7:7
Deliver You	130	Psalm 50:15
Deliverance	30	Isaiah 26:18

INDEX

Name	Page	Scripture
Deliverer, My	129	Psalm 18:2
Discerns the Righteous One	137	Jeremiah 20:12
Does Not Retain His Anger	84	Micah 7:18
Door, The	63	John 10:7
Elect, My	47	Isaiah 42:1
Eminence of Israel	180	1 Samuel 15:29
Endures Forever	174	Psalm 136:16
Erases Your Transgressions	86	Isaiah 43:25
Eternal King	173	1 Timothy 1:17
Everlasting Father	45	Isaiah 9:5
Everlasting God	174	Genesis 21:33
Exalted	157	Isaiah 5:16
Examines Minds and Hearts	97	Revelation 2:23
Executes Loving Kindness and Justice	89	Psalm 103:6
Eyes, His	12	2 Chronicles 16:9
Eyes, Seven	12	Zechariah 3:9
Eyes, Seven Are	12	Zechariah 4:8-10
Executing Judgment	99	Deuteronomy 10:18
Face to Face	140	Genesis 32:30
Faithful and True Witness	39	Revelation 3:14
Father	75	Matthew 6:9
Father, My	74	Jeremiah 3:19
Father, One	75	Malachi 2:10
Father, Our	75	Isaiah 63:16
Father, Your	74	Deuteronomy 32:6
Favor Leaders, Does Not	87	Job 34:19
Fight for You	119	Exodus 14:14
First	37	Colossians 1:18
First and Last	39	Isaiah 41:4

Name	Page	Scripture
Help You	144	Isaiah 41:13
Helper	144	Hebrews 13:6
Hiding Place, My	132	Psalm 119:114
High Tower, My	129	Psalm 18:2
Holy God	161	1 Samuel 6:20
Holy One	162	Habakkuk 3:3
Holy One of Israel	162	2 Kings 19:22
Holy One, The	162	1 John 2:20
Holy Ones	163	Proverbs 9:10
Hope of Israel	48	Jeremiah 14:8
Hope of Israel, The	49	Acts 28:20
Horn of My Salvation	129	Psalm 18:2
Hoshea-na, Hosanna	30	Matthew 21:9
Humble	53	Zechariah 9:9
Husband	43	Joshua 5:13
Husband	77	Genesis 32:25
Husband, My	76	Hosea 2:16
Husband, Your	76	Isaiah 54:5
I AM	72	Exodus 3:14
I AM	73	Genesis 15:1
I AM	73	Genesis 17:7
I AM	43	Matthew 14:27
I AM Who I AM	72	Exodus 3:14
I Have Walked	141	2 Samuel 7:7
Image	5	2 Corinthians 4:3,4
I Will Be With You	141	Deuteronomy 31:23
I Will Send Grain, Wine, & Oil	104	Joel 2:19
Imanuel	42	Isaiah 7:14
Immortal	173	1 Timothy 1:17
Inheritance, Your	155	Numbers 18:20
Invisible	173	1 Timothy 1:17

Name	Page	Scripture
Light	36	Psalm 119:105
Light, My	151	Psalm 27:1
Light, The	37	John 1:7
Lights, Father of	151	James 1:17
Lion of the Tribe of Judah	57	Revelation 5:5
Living God	72	Joshua 3:10
Living God	72	Daniel 6:27
Living One, The	37	Revelation 1:17,18
Lord God	4	Ezekiel 3:11
Lord, My	96	Genesis 15:2
Lord of All	55	Acts 10:36
Lord of Glory	44	1 Corinthians 2:8
Lord of Hosts	118	1 Samuel 1:3
Lord of Hosts	38	Revelation 1:8
Lord of Kings	95	Daniel 2:47
Lord of Lords	95	Deuteronomy 10:17
Lord of Lords	40	Revelation 17:14
Lord of Lords	41	Revelation 19:16
Lord of the Harvest, The	60	Matthew 9:38
Lord of the Lords	94	1 Timothy 6:15
Lord of the Sabbath	60	Matthew 12:8
Lord, The	147	Jeremiah 16:21
Love	80	1 John 4:7,8
Loves	80	John 16:27
Loves Justice	96	Isaiah 61:8
Made Pleiades and Orion	111	Amos 5:8
Made You	115	Isaiah 44:2
Majesty	94	Hebrews 8:1
Make Mankind	114	Genesis 1:26
Make Peace	112	Isaiah 45:7
Maker of Heavens and Earth	113	Psalm 124:8
Maker, My	116	Job 35:10,11

INDEX

Name	Page	Scripture
Maker, Your	110	Isaiah 51:12,13
Makes Us Wiser	116	Job 35:10,11
Man	77	Genesis 32:25
Man of Your Right Hand	46	Psalm 80:18
Man, The	74	1 Chronicles 17:16,17
Man of War	118	Exodus 15:3
Mashiakh, The	56	John 1:41
Mashiakh Prince	56	Daniel 9:25
Master	61	Luke 8:24
Master, The	61	2 Peter 2:1
Mediator	66	1 Timothy 2:5
Messiah	55	Matthew 1:16
Messiah, My	56	Psalm 132:17
Messiah, The	55	Mark 15:31,32
Midst	141	Numbers 35:34
Might, Spirit of	14	Isaiah 11:1,2
Mighty God	45	Isaiah 9:5
Mighty in Strength	136	Job 9:4
Mighty One of Israel	180	Isaiah 1:24
Mighty One of Jacob	31	Genesis 49:24
Minister	67	Hebrews 8:2
Miracle	35	Judges 13:18
Miracle, My	106	Exodus 17:15
Most High God	92	Genesis 14:18
Name	29	Acts 5:28
Name, The	147	Deuteronomy 28:58
One	3	Deuteronomy 6:4
One	148	Zechariah 14:9
One Ruling	41	Micah 5:2
Only God	3	1 Timothy 1:17
Only Wise God	135	Romans 16:27

Name	Page	Scripture
Savior	48	Jeremiah 14:8
Savior	66	Philippians 3:20
Savior, Our	131	1 Timothy 1:1
Savior, Your	132	Isaiah 43:3
Search the Heart	97	Jeremiah 17:10
Seed	65	Galatians 3:16
Seed, The	65	Galatians 3:19
Seek Out My Sheep	88	Ezekiel 34:12
Sees Innermost Thoughts and Feelings	137	Jeremiah 20:12
Servant, My	47	Isaiah 42:1
Shakes the Earth, He Who	103	Job 9:6
Shepherd	31	Genesis 49:24
Shepherd, My	48	Zechariah 13:7
Shepherd, The Chief	33	1 Peter 5:4
Shepherd, The Good	32	John 10:11
Shepherd, The Great	32	Hebrews 13:20
Shield	125	Genesis 15:1
Shield, Our	125	Psalm 59:11
Shiloh	28	Genesis 49:10
Shoot	45	Isaiah 11:1
Sign	106	Isaiah 11:10
Son, My	59	Matthew 2:15
Son, My	60	Hosea 11:1
Son of Abraham	58	Matthew 1:1
Son of David	59	Matthew 15:22
Son of the Living God, The	60	Matthew 16:16
Son of Man	46	Psalm 80:18
Son of Man	47	Daniel 7:13
Son of Man	60	Matthew 12:8
Son of the Most High	60	Luke 1:32
Song	149	Exodus 15:2

Name	Page	Scripture
Understanding, Spirit of	14	Isaiah 11:1
Upright One	50	Isaiah 26:7
Vengeance, God of	125	Psalm 94:1
Vengeance, Lord God of	125	Psalm 94:1
Vengeance Against His Foes	126	Nahum 1:2
Victories	29	2 Samuel 22:51
Wage War for You	119	Deuteronomy 3:22
Walked, I Have	141	2 Samuel 7:7
Way of the Lord	167	Genesis 18:19
Way of the Lord	167	Acts 18:25
Way, Truth, and Life, The	63	John 14:6
Welfare	30	Job 30:15
Well, Living One My Seer	8	Genesis 24:62
Well, Living One Seeing Me	8	Genesis 16:14
Who Brings Good News	57	Nahum 2:1
Who Commands the Sun	105	Job 9:7
Who Was and Who Is Coming	174	Revelation 1:4
Will Deliver	129	1 Samuel 17:47
Will Hold Your Right Hand	144	Isaiah 41:13
Wisdom, Spirit of	14	Isaiah 11:1,2
Wise of Heart	136	Job 9:4
With Us, God Is	42	Isaiah 7:14
With You	43	Matthew 28:19,20
With You	139	Genesis 21:22
With You, I AM	141	Haggai 1:13
With You, I Will Be	141	Deuteronomy 31:23
Witness	136	Jeremiah 29:23
Witness, My, Attester, My	136	Job 16:19
Witness, Faithful	68	Revelation 1:5
Witness, Faithful and True	39	Revelation 3:14

Receive your FREE e-version of William Morford's book:
God's Rythm of Life: Seasons of The Lord. Understanding the
Jewish Roots of the Church.
Visit: www.OneNewManBible.com/Seasons